A New Age-Scale
for Humans

A New Age-Scale for Humans

WITHDRAWN

Daniel Hershey
Hsuan-Hsien Wang
University of Cincinnati

LexingtonBooks
D.C. Heath and Company
Lexington, Massachusetts
Toronto

Library of Congress Cataloging in Publication Data

Hershey, Daniel.
  A new age-scale for humans.

  Bibliography: p.
  Includes index.
  1. Aging. 2. Longevity. 3. Metabolism. 4. Entropy.
I. Wang, Hsuan-Hsien, joint author. II. Title.
QP86.H49   612.6'7   79–8318
ISBN 0–669–03374–x

Published simultaneously in Canada.

Printed in the United States of America.

International Standard Book Number: 0–669–03374–x

Library of Congress Catalog Card Number: 79–8318

Contents

List of Figures

List of Tables

Preface

Everyone is interested in aging. Scientists cannot ignore the changes occurring daily as we humans evolve from birth to maturity, senescence, and death. Therefore, we have read and learned and attempted to make sense of a plethora of facts and figures in books and journals spanning an awesome range of disciplines. From a background of chemical engineering, thermodynamics, physiology, and biology, we have produced this book on why we age, the factors affecting aging, the parameters for measuring it, and, most importantly, a new age-scale for humans. We have also included a simple design for a whole-body calorimeter for obtaining the basal metabolic rate data needed to calculate our new metabolic or entropy age.

Where will all this lead? We hope it will lead to the end of the tyranny of the clock, to the end of the overuse of chronological age as a measure of our worth—a measure by which our lives are directed unreasonably.

1 Aging and Evolving of Systems

If only we could remain the same, you and I, youthful and strong, resilient and hopeful, ever-learning, never weary, always able to rebound to meet the next day. We express the plea for a status quo, a steady state, but only if conditions are perfect or nearly perfect for us. For some, the goal is not to remain unchanged, not to continue repeating in some way that which is our present lot. No, the aim is for evolution, an ascendancy from the present to the future during which we will raise our station in life, improve our health if this is important, make more money, raise a family, build a house—do whatever is required to make the transition.

The governing boards of corporations strive for increased profits with diminished expenses and larger sales generated by a curtailed, more efficient work force. There is pride in announcing that more plants are being built and the corporation is growing. In other words, corporations deplore a status quo situation, through fear that caviling stockholders will interpret a steady state as a static state and attach to it a negative connotation. Countries, like corporations, pride themselves on ever-increasing gross national profits, eschewing any interest in limiting production. There is the feeling that bigger is better, that a cessation in the upward spiral is tantamount to stagnation and stagnation leads to senescence; and we all know that civilizations decline and die.

So there are different philosophies at work. Do you ascribe to the steady-state or the evolving-state doctrine? Do you prefer to remain close to some sort of equilibrium condition and allow that small perturbations can be handled in a way that returns us to our original state? Do you regard with suspicion those who proclaim there is an entrenched, privileged class and an oppressive bureaucratic structure which must be torn asunder in order to build anew from the ashes of the old? Are there those who see change as not only possible but necessary for the orderly transition—the gradual evolution—from one stable state to another? Of course, there are persons who seek change for all these and other reasons. Each group representing another philosophy exerts its own pressures on the structure. The changes sought may be for the better or may be disastrous, depending on the goals and whether we can control the change agents to some extent.

Thus we have a dilemma. Is the life of a living system, such as a human being, to be seen as a wear-and-tear process as the individual winds down, or is it a gradual evolution from birth through intermediate states to matu-

1

rity, senescence, and death. Death is inevitable for all living organisms. For structures such as corporations, it is not readily apparent that they age and die, though some will go bankrupt, which is a form of death. Civilizations die in some way. There have been golden ages for Greece and Rome and perhaps even for the United States. Who can say that the forces at work on civilizations are not similar to those which stress a living human system.

To aver that there are various change possibilities for a system (see figure 1-1) is of course to state the obvious. The changes can take a number of forms such as that shown in figure 1-1a. This is called a neutrally stable condition. Place yourself on one of the closed loops and allow that things will change in such a way as to trace a path on the line, always maintaining a circumscribed series of states. There are limits to the deviations and under no circumstances are conditions sufficient to drive you off the line. In this world the perturbations from equilibrium never get out of control. If the speed on a highway is 55 miles per hour and you are law abiding, you might average that speed yet there will be times when you travel at 60 or 50. But you always strive to return to the speed limit. Perhaps you can think of other examples. The earth in its rotation around the sun traces an orbit which is cyclic and predictable, and is an example of a neutrally stable state.

On the other hand, some systems behave in a manner called unstable equilibrium (see figure 1-1b). Here is a situation where starting from state A changes occur, but instead of cycling in a fixed orbit as before, now there is a movement way from the initial condition, a spiraling departure from the home base. Not only is the system deviating markedly from the original state, but it is seemingly changing at an accelerated pace, heading toward what may be disaster. This could be the case of a poorly designed nuclear reactor, one with improper temperature control. The heat generated by the nuclear reaction stimulates an increasing rate of reaction which yields additional heat which boosts the reaction rate further, developing still more heat, and so on. Or perhaps we are tracing the loss of middle-class persons from the inner cities. With the departure of some, the tax bite increases for those who remain, schools deteriorate, crime increases, and more middle-class persons flee to the suburbs. This then continues the exacerbation of the initial problem—only now the level of intensity of the difficulty has been raised and more flights occur. Gradually, steadily, conditions escalate and we head toward a seemingly doomed situation unless there is outside intervention or the constituents themselves can change the pattern.

But there are still other possibilities for systems to change; one possibility is referred to as stable equilibrium, a condition which allows the system to converge toward a well-defined end point (see figure 1-1c). From starting state A, given proper driving forces, the organization will change—as do the others already discussed—but now the amplitude of change is controlled and confined to ever-narrowing levels until finally all pressures lead to one

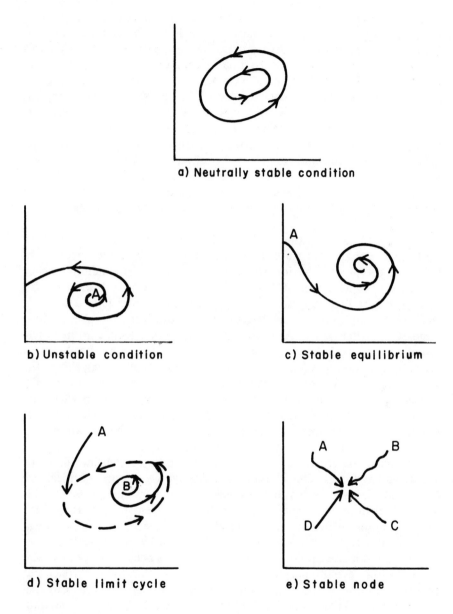

a) Neutrally stable condition

b) Unstable condition

c) Stable equilibrium

d) Stable limit cycle

e) Stable node

Figure 1–1. Change Possibilities for a Living Human System

stable, unyielding position. Some negotiations between persons, or other complex organizations (such as successful collective bargaining sessions), trace out such a history. In this example, there is a narrowing of differences and a graceful evolution toward a final state, a compromise. Such system behavior usually is aided by inherent moderating influences which prevent blowups; that is, they prevent an uncontrolled growth of the stresses or change agents. It is as if the system were being reined in relentlessly by forces outside it. Some people believe our universe is an example of such a system, where attractive forces between matter are unyielding in drawing galactic bodies closer and closer. As the universe condenses, to follow the logic a bit further, there is the likelihood of disaster for with the atomic packing, it may reach a state of critical mass density which yields a big explosion—the big-bang theory-and another cycle of an expanding universe may be initiated.

Finally, to complete this list of possibilities for system behavior, there are two more modes: the stable limit cycle and the stable node. Figure 1-1d illustrates a type of behavior where the neutrally stable condition can be arrived at from a number of different starting conditions (A and B in this sketch). Figure 1-1e suggests that the system may converge to a constant final condition (a stable node) despite a history of diverse initial conditions imposed upon the system. A spring-wound pendulum clock, starting at rest (point B in figure 1-1d), will commence to hunt for its final stable limit cycle. Should the pendulum be given an unusually large starting shove, the system would in effect be starting from point A in figure 1-1d and gradually descend toward the same stable limit cycle. A spinning top, no matter what initial velocity imposed, will always end at rest, a mode of behavior illustrated in figure 1-1e. Death as the ultimate end is approached by all of us in different ways, but the preordained fey conclusion is the same.

We sense the growth within a fixed structure must run into limits or countervailing forces. The dinosaur probably evolved toward a critical size beyond which it was impossible to support the immense body weight. This increased girth could have affected the dinosaur lifespan by causing difficulty in finding sufficient food to sustain life. Some systems or organizations are able to adapt in a stepwise fashion via different structural states and find an ultimate equilibrium. The cockroach is believed to be an example of such an evolutionary process; it is thought that the cockroach has changed very little in the long history that humans have observed this species. Further cockroach development is seemingly foreclosed by its equilibrium teleological state.

But there are those who propose system descriptions and analyses which depart from equilibrium assessments, and enter the arcane world of nonequilibrium (dissipative) states. Instead of seeking the security of constancy, these proponents of nonequilibrium dynamics say that organizations proceed to and through various plateaus, resting on each level until displaced by the convergent forces of energy, material, and information exchange with the environment. The human body can be seen anew in this light; humans maintain a relatively stable state until an illness changes their lives. A corporation operates under known, relatively constant conditions until it merges with another corporation. And so it goes, these open systems are capable of being driven from one seemingly stable orbit of operations into another. The system attempts to remain viable by switching to a new dynamic regime yielding, in a sense, order through fluctuations, which is the reverse of the behavior of some systems near equilibrium. The organizations near equilibrium attempt to meet new pressures for change by damping them out and returning to their original conditions after small, temporary deviations. Some might claim the forces of racial integration were like this, where for a while, the integrationists' pressures were met by sufficient resistance to continue the original segregated condition. There seemed to be stability in the segregated state but this was specious since the time frame was not sufficiently long to see the trends. Actually, the segregated state was inherently unstable. When the forces for integration became morally irresistible, the system moved to a new nonequilibrium position, which is the present point in history. Thus instead of having a civil war over the issue, society found order through fluctuation or change. In the new state of nonequilibrium, order may increase, and in this state our response to old pressures is met with more degrees of freedom. There are more ways to meet old problems. With the new dynamics of order through fluctuations, the challenge is to delineate the bounds of stability and to attempt to identify the new state in which we are or to which we wish to go. There can be surprises along the way, of course. For example, a system can be driven too far in size and complexity, as some think New York City has been. The high density of the population and the limited system of roads in Manhattan has led to the surprising result that it is often quicker to walk across Manhattan than it is to drive the same distance in an automobile.

These dissipative, nonequilibrium states might in some simple cases be described by mathematical equations with appropriate feedback relationships (figure 1–2). If the feedback is negative (figure 1–2a), this feedback or return of knowledge and information to the pressure point is considered a control on the pressure fluctuation. The tendency is toward stability and a subsiding of the system to its original state. (The negative values of feedback help neutralize positive pressures.) Should the feedback be positive (figure 1–2b), we have a condition where there is reinforcement of the amplitude of the fluctuations. (We add a positive pressure to a positive feedback.) This yields a higher output, increasing the positive feedback value, which when added to the positive pressure gives a still larger output.

Presumably a point could be reached where the sheer size of the fluctu-

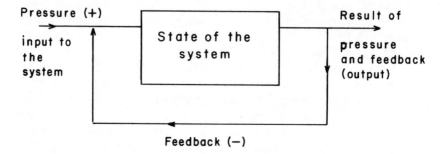

(a) Negative feedback

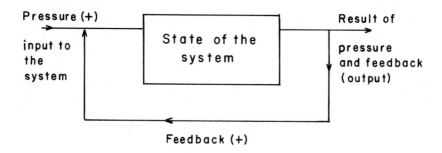

(b) Positive feedback

Figure 1-2. Dissipative, Nonequilibrium States with Feedback Relationships

ation drives the system to a new plateau and a new nonequilibrium or dissipative structure. To use a chemical example, if we are watching a chemical reaction and suddenly the temperature of the reaction vessel deviates from the set temperature, it is possible that a new unexpected substance may be produced along with the usual material. Should the new product begin to diminish in concentration or remain the same as the desired temperature is restored, then everything will operate to reinstate the initial conditions. However, should the concentration of the new unexpected product start to increase when proper temperatures are restored, there is a likelihood that this amplification of the perturbation will lead to a new set of chemical reactions and hence move the original state to a new plateau where the chemistry is different and the products are not what we planned.

Whether considering organizations such as corporations, societal structures such as the welfare system, human living organisms, or the universe, what emerges is a general schema for change, a way of going from one nonequilibrium state (of disorder) to the next nonequilibrium state: order through fluctuations. We get there by deviation-amplifying or positive-feedback means. This might be called a revitalization process, requiring explicit intent by members of society. To get there from here, the system needs to go through these steps: (1) achieve a nonequilibrium plateau, (2) experience stress, (3) endure cultural distortion, (4) plan for revitalization, and (5) enter a new nonequilibrium plateau. The manager of such a system is the catalyst rather than the designer of an organization. The task of management under nonequilibrium conditions is to stimulate the growth of a network of decision processes. One objective of this network would be to maintain or renew the autonomous unity of the organization. In other words, it becomes imperative for proper functioning of an organization to allow and guarantee the various integral parts of the system their degrees of freedom within the constraints of the planned operating mode. With the network in place, and with the long-term goals and a timetable for the organization in mind, management's function becomes linked with procedures for producing components within the organization capable of recursively regenerating the network.

Social theories have traditionally been geared to structure, not process, and to ideals of equilibrium and structural stability (stable equilibrium). The emphasis has been on steady state and negative feedback (which corrects deviations). It may be that the analysis and planning of social organizations now may need to be brought into consonance with the newer nonequilibrium order through fluctuations approach. Contemporary society is characterized by a rapid dissemination of information. In the past, science and technology were the chief agents of positive feedback (deviations from existing norms were amplified) in transforming human-environment relationships, while societal philosophy and techniques provided negative feedback to stabilize the relationships. But the deviation-amplifying process can increase differentiation, develop structure, and generate complexity. This may work to enrich society and allow us to move on to something better than we had previously. A basic principle of the biological and social universe seems to be that we tend toward diversification, heterogeneity, and symbiotization (the close relationship of two or more systems). What survives is not necessarily the strongest, but the most symbiotic. We may have been misguided by traditional scientific logic into believing generalizability, universality, homogenization, and competition are not only the rulers of the universe but also the desirable goals for society. Much of the unpredictability of history is perhaps attributable to deviation-amplifying causes. The result is either a runaway situation or evolution.

2 On Time

The past no longer exists. The future has not arrived yet, but there is a need to plan for it. The present is reality.

Is time the prime reality as the Greeks believed, an independent and relentless power, destroying everything like an all-devouring monster? Time heals all wounds we say, implying an inherently good power; on the other hand, the degenerative wear-and-tear processes which yield ultimate death proceed with time as we are painfully aware. Time is associated with events like birth, death, growth, and decay.

Cause and Effect: Before and After

To attempt to understand time, we must explore the meaning of *before* and *after* and that syllogism which says because of *A* (which we observe) *B* was caused to happen, and therefore we conclude that *B* came after *A*. But how do you measure the event which is *A*? It's easy, we say. For example, it's a simple matter to observe the lightning flash in the sky and a moment later hear the thunderclap. So it is; but how long did it take for the light of the lightning bolt to reach our eyes? And from where did it begin? We know that sound waves travel more slowly than light—1,000 feet per second compared to 186,000 miles per second—which means that the thunderclap will arrive at our ears later than the registering of the lightning flash in the eye, even though both are generated at the exact same instant. The closer the observer is to the lightning, the more simultaneous are the recordings of the occurrence. And as we all know, for one who is unfortunately in the immediate vicinity of the lightning, it is difficult for the unaided observer to tell which came first, the light or the sound.

The Form of Time

The early Greek philosophers raised the question of the structure of time: is time continuous or discontinuous; that is, can we divide time into an infinite number of ever-so-small intervals (continuous time) or is there some limited size of the discrete time interval, which implies a discontinuous march of time. Often time is considered a flow, as a river might flow, with a clearly defined direction. But rivers can be blocked, and major events can cause waterways to change direction and perhaps even reverse themselves. Can time be reversed? Is time therefore a physical reality—something tangible—or is it a psychological phenomenon, possessing no corporeal mass and related to and altered by our perceptions of it? Common sense might dictate that the rate of flow or movement of time is constant: a second is a second and an hour is an hour. But is a day a day and what does this mean? Physicists say that time marches on at a rate determined by circumstances, especially when huge cosmic distances or very high velocities are involved. If we define time as motion measured, such as "it took me 8 minutes to run the mile," then how are we to know when we are at the starting point and where is the end? Couldn't we take photographs at the start and end (when there is no motion), but how would we tell the time? On the other hand, if we photograph a person in youth and later in adulthood, it will be apparent that time has passed and, additionally, it should be easy to establish which is the earlier photograph.

Some say there are at least two theories of time, one that time is a product of the mind while physical things and places are timeless or, alternatively, time is not dependent on our thought processes; it exists as an independent reality, its presence real and unconnected with efforts to observe it. The first statement attempts to make the point that we have defined a concept. So we know an hour has passed when by definition the clock ticks off 3,600 intervals, and when the earth circles the sun we call that 1 day with 24 hours. But the second theory means the obverse, that time exists in its own right as a tangible entity whose comprehension only awaits our ascending evolutionary development. At the proper stage in our history we shall, as Arthur Clark wrote in his story *2001*, be able to fully understand what it is that we now call time. In the meantime we shall simply have to muddle along measuring and observing time's passage and building more and more sophisticated devices to indirectly record its existence.

The philosophers John Locke, David Hume and Rene Descartes considered the succession of ideas in the mind as the origin of our concept of time. We think, therefore we are—and in so doing define the ebb and flow of events, ordering them in relation to our mind's eye picture of our finite ambience and, by extension, the infinite universe. Or are we like someone on a boat in a river of time, floating through the countryside? Which is the true reality here? Is time the river or the permanent, stationary riverbank? And are there more rivers elsewhere, cutting through other countrysides? Perhaps our concept of past, present, and future has significance only in human thought and is in reality merely an anthropocentric idea, invented by humans to satisfy a need to be at the center of things.

The Measurement of Time

Time's measurement may be derived from a series of successive experiences, each anchored to a benchmark or point of reference. The procession from one benchmark to the next would define the passage of time, much as in a horse race when the lead horse passes first the quarter-mile pole, then the half-mile pole, and so on. But there is nothing new here, for the benchmarks still require us to know *the* time, suggesting that the concept of time is innate. As usual, and we should expect it by now, there is some evidence which seemingly contradicts the notion that time has an innateness: several kinds of animals—for example, birds, insects, and even humans—possess something called an internal or biological clock which is adaptable to changing environmental conditions. So in the spring when we move our clocks forward 1 hour in the parts of the United States where daylight saving time is practiced, the inhabitants adjust and go to bed an hour earlier than usual and awaken an hour later. Within a day or two we don't give this change a second thought. Seemingly, nothing has changed.

Returning for a moment to the imagery of time flowing as a river, suppose we in our mind remove the river shoreline and visualize time again as a great river but now self-contained, capable of flowing without confining shoreline boundaries. This immense stream without visible banks contains all there is, all that exists, floating on it. At certain moments, which here are specific locations in the river, each of us as a floating object sinks and disappears and hence no longer exists. Time flies, we say. What we really mean is time flows. All of us and everything that defines our existence are seen floating along, capable of holding our own for just so long before the river overwhelms our capabilities and we submerge.

It is the before-after logical chain which seems to be at the core of the discussion of time, for even the gravest cases of mental illness, patients utterly disoriented as to the time of day, can still tell whether a sound precedes or follows a light signal. The concept of time may have arisen when we became conscious of our reactions to certain sensations, so that first there were feelings (before) and then we acted (after). Or is it the other way? There is a belief that time is a series of events, that time as a concept was first founded on our ability to distinguish the sounds of these occurrences. But then the inevitable question is raised: what if we were insulated from sound?

Isolated events have no place in time, say some philosophers who propose that these events are not to be considered as pieces of wood floating in a time river. Instead, they say, why not compare time with the molecules of water which compose the river. Passing water molecules become the flow of time in this view. Time does not exist; it only flows. Thus the meaning of time has shifted from a flow of discrete events to a flow of a medium (a river) in which events take place or have a place.

Though descriptions and definitions of time have not yet become focused, we still must work with time. To measure time, we need, first of all, to recognize or accept one simple paradigm; that is, time may be considered a sequence of events (though this sequence is not yet clearly ascertained). Next we choose a partial sequence which may be representative of the all-embracing one. We call such a partial sequence a clock. So the winding down of a spring in such a device approximates the 24-hour day, which in turn approximates the regularity of the movement of earth, sun, and stars. These heavenly body movements are assumed to be models of the behavior of other galaxies and, hence, the universe as a whole. To say one's sense of time is relative is to relate it to our own experience, where an interval of time in which many things happen is felt to be much longer than another interval of the same length in which almost nothing happens. True sometimes. But based on experimental evidence, we know that we must factor into these results the allowance that it is not only this information content but also the complexity of the information which affects our sense of time flow. Not only does the information content and its complexity guide or control our impressions, but, additionally, doesn't it make sense to expect that this availability of information requires on the observer's part an activated or receptive state. So for small children, up to about age 5, to tell them that something is to occur soon (in a week) needs some concretization. They understand better when we tell them that after they have gone to bed and awakened seven times, the week will be up. In earlier times we measured time by the rising and setting sun or the appearance of the moon. Time was experienced in the periodicity and rhythms in our lives as well as in the life cycles in nature. Thus was invented the sundial, and Stonehenge and our present-day clocks with faces and hands. We designed devices to measure the duration of events, such as the so-called hourglass (in which sand flows through a constriction at a controlled rate) and the burning of a candle. Today we are a bit more sophisticated and utilize sidereal clocks which are based on the movement of stars and, by implication, relate time to our galaxy motion. There are light clocks which measure the distance traveled by light and pendulum clocks with their oscillating arms traversing distances at fixed-time intervals. Atomic clocks measure the vibrations in an atom of cesium.

The Direction of Time

There is only one time but many different types of clocks for measuring the partial sequence we designate as a time interval. Some liken the flow of time not to the flow of a river but to the flow of words. And if we cannot or do not "think" in words, does this imply no movement of time? Of course not. What is being suggested by the word-flow proponents is a return to the theory that time relates to our mental processes. Here we have the proposition that time was invented to account for a flow of a river (or torrent) of words and thoughts. If older people feel that the days of their youth were shorter than current days, is it true that time "flies" when we are busy; time "crawls" when we are bored. Then can the rate of flow of time be tied to the total number of events in the whole universe? Is the flow of time constant, infinite, indeterminant? One thing we believe we do know: the rate of flow of time cannot be negative. In other words, time's flows—forward and backward—are not equivalent. Time flows from past to future (or from earlier to later), and should we be able to reverse things and look at the future going to the past, we would not have an exact repetition of the process. For example, show a film in the correct sequence and then run the machine backward. It's true we'll end up where we started but everyone and everything shown will be moving unnaturally and usually in violation of some accepted natural laws, such as dropped objects ascending unaided in violation of the law of gravity. A heavy body always falls down; heat always flows from the hot side of something to the cold. From these cases do we infer a direction for time: event A (the release of the heavy object) is always followed by event B (the fall of the object). Therefore A is the cause of B and A is earlier than B. What we are dealing with here is the observation that in nature there is a general tendency toward leveling; local differences tend to become spontaneously smaller and eventually disappear. The object, hot on one side and cold on the other, if allowed to stand untouched will show heat flow from the hot side to the cold side, the temperature difference will diminish with time, and eventually the entire object will be at the same temperature.

There is an inclination of every system to pass from a highly ordered, less probably state to a less ordered, more probably one. For example, such a highly ordered, less probable state might be a tank containing a gas under pressure. Open the valve on the tank and the gas molecules will spread into the surroundings and become mixed with the ambient air molecules. The new mixed condition is more usual or probable and less organized or ordered than is the initial high-pressure state. Given no interference, the tendency is always for the high-pressure gas to flow out of the tank. The more randomly things are distributed, the more likely is that state. The most probable state is characterized by maximum disorder or randomness. Spontaneous processes (the tank emptying, the heat flow from the hot to the cold surface, the dropped object falling to the ground) proceed in a way which may be considered to delineate the direction of time.

Having introduced the idea of events proceeding in one direction only, governed by seemingly immutable laws related to probability and order, this seems like the propitious moment (in time?) to bring up an arcane, artificial concept: entropy. Derived from the so-called hard sciences of physics, chemistry, and engineering, entropy can be defined as a measure of the randomness or disorder of a system and is related to its information content. Processes proceeding spontaneously (remember the gas in the cylinder, the heat flow, and the fall of a heavy object examples) are said to go irreversibly for they cannot of their own volition return to their original conditions. Such one-sided events march from a more ordered to a less ordered state. They go in the direction from low probability to high probability. In entropy terms, we say they proceed in the direction of increasing entropy. So increasing entropy is associated with increasing disorder which corresponds to the most probable state. Now we have another possible way of specifying the direction of the flow of time: unaided, natural processes head in the direction of increasing entropy, tending in the final analysis toward a state of maximum entropy. Even that ultimate of irreversible processes—the course of human life, the aging process—proceeds with increasing entropy and its concomitant disorder.

Previously we said that time was tied to the observation of events. Time's arrow was seemingly connected to the before-after sequence, which allowed us to assess the direction of time flow. But there remains a nagging question which must be faced, having to do with whether it might be possible for observers to see a series of events in different order. Is the direction of time the same throughout the universe? What we mean by a reversal of the direction of time is that the later events take place sooner, so that for the vase which fell and broke—now the pieces are observed to fly upward and join to form the original vase. This is clearly impossible to accomplish unaided, at least so far as our present knowledge dictates. A partial reversal of the direction of time would seem unlikely (only the vase and nothing else in our world may repair itself spontaneously). It's all or nothing it would seem; either the entire universe is capable of time reversal or nothing is. If time reversal could occur, all laws of nature would keep their validity and the whole world would run through the exact same states as before, only in the reverse order of succession. Somehow this seems logically impossible. But perhaps it is wrong to dismiss this question of reversibility so facilely. If we think of time reversal as a reversal of the motion of elementary particles such as electrons and other parts of atoms, it may indeed be possible for these particles to pass through exactly the same states as before. In other words, we say there is the possibility of microscopic reversibility, but macroscopic systems (the whole which is composed of these elementary particles) such as the falling object and the gas in the cylinder cannot be made to run unaided through the exact same sequence of states as before, but in the reverse order of succession.

Time's Duration

Time is relative in some respects. Here relative means being dependent on something else. The theory of relativity from physics holds that the duration of an interval between two events is dependent upon the state of motion of the observer. To an observer at rest this interval would be longer than it would be to an observer in motion. Still another difficulty in ascertaining the direction and duration of time has to do with the problem of establishing simultaneity. In other words, how can you tell when two events occur exactly at the same moment. For example, the simultaneity of events on two distant stars is difficult to establish. On earth it would seem easier to do since the distances are smaller, and the light or electronic signal which conveys our information travels at such astronomical velocities. But a happening on a star might be observed many years after its occurrence. Not only that, but the velocity of light is not always known exactly, for the light rays can be deflected by a heavy body such as a star.

The theory of relativity says that temporal or time relationships and the events we measure do not exist independently, by themselves, but are linked temporarily to an observer. The "instant" when an event occurs is localized and can be different in different places. From physics we know that a clock in motion runs slower than a clock at rest. Now we've added the complication of the motion of the clock and the observer to all the other problems in establishing when events occurred in distant stars—and in defining time and its direction (if it does indeed have a direction). Perhaps what we measure with a clock isn't all that accurate anyway, but is specious. Consider the case of the hypothetical space traveler. The traveler departs from earth in a rocket at or near the speed of light and on the return appears to have aged much less than those who remained on earth. The explanation of the puzzle is usually given in terms of the difference in the time interval experienced by the space traveler and the earth dweller. We are measuring things with two nonsynchronous clocks; one goes with the rocket at or near the speed of light and the other remains on earth and moves at a lesser velocity. The two clocks tick off different time intervals: the cumulative time interval for the space traveler is less than for the earthbound.

As speed increases, time seems to slow. If we were able to achieve speeds equal to the speed of light, equations predict that time would finally stand still. Recently new elementary particles have been discovered and labeled tachyons. These tachyons are believed to move faster than the speed of light. If this is true, can we say that for the tachyons time flows backward since they travel faster than the limiting velocity—the speed of light—where time stands still. This is probably an absurd conclusion to draw so there must be other possibilities. One alternative hypothesizes that tachyons are entirely different particles than the usual ones and for them the limit is still the speed of light but they approach this boundary from the other side, coming down in velocity toward the speed of light. Most particles and systems we have experienced approach the speed of light from below.

There is still the question of whether time is continuous or discontinuous. If time is continuous, it can be divided into an infinite number of infinitesimal intervals. Or is time discontinuous and hence can only consist of discrete atoms or quanta of finite duration. If time is continuous, is it like a line; the line, we say, is composed of an infinite number of points. If time were discontinuous and composed of discrete moments, do the moments touch? How long is each moment? What do we call the space between moments if they don't touch? Time periods smaller than 10^{-22} seconds (0.0000000000000000000001 second) cannot be measured today and as a consequence we have no idea whether a time moment can be less than this. The smallest increment of space which can be measured, a so-called space quantum, consists of 10^{-15} meters (0.000000000000001 meter) where a meter is 100 centimeters or a little more than a yard in length. If both time and space consist of quanta, perhaps fuzzy in appearance so that it is difficult to tell where one ends and the next begins, only extremely close observations could yield a flow of time which appeared to be discontinuous. Most events in everyday life are measured no closer than a hundredth of a second (10^{-2} or 0.01 second) and time therefore would seem continuous because of our inability to distinguish the exact boundary between earlier and later quanta of time. By assuming the quanta to be fuzzy and fading into each other, we can neatly avoid the need to choose which model of time we prefer: the continuous or discontinuous one. We can visualize particles gliding continuously from one time quanta into the next. These quanta can be compared with droplets of liquid. Droplets can coalesce to form a continuum, which is one of the proposed models for the flow of time.

Cyclic Time

Of course, time could also be cyclic and if you believe this, the universe will have to retrace its past steps and go through the same series of events. The proponents of the cyclic theory ask, why must we assume that time had a beginning as do the linear time thinkers. Why would the first event in our history occur? Why should time have an end? Shouldn't time be infinite at both ends of its boundary, in the past and future? These cyclic time believers say there is nothing in our experience which supports the view that there has ever been a first event or that there will be a last. Hence why couldn't time be cyclic, returning to its original state again and again. During one cycle we trace out a history and return to the beginning. Then the history unfolds again. In essence there is no beginning or end in this model. Thus if the universe were awakened from its deathlike rest once by a big bang, why not a second time and a third time and so on. If moments of time have no identity in themselves but owe their character to the events which take place at them, the cyclic theory of time implies a cyclic theory of events. But with cycles, if a particular moment begins a cycle, it can be perceived as being before every other moment. It becomes a matter of definition: where do we choose to begin the cycle. If we wish, we could arrange the cycle so that a particular moment comes after every other moment. But with this latitude comes the possibility that an effect could precede its cause, allowing such unreasonable conclusions as death could preceded birth. With this logical difficulty to be faced, is it any wonder that the cyclic theory of time has few followers?

Conclusions

In summary, time has to do with events. Time is a primitive relationship; it is a product of the mind but based on the reality of physical bodies and what happens to them. Time is infinite and may or may not be continuous. Temporal or time relationships are between changes of the state of bodies. Time has only one dimension. One can travel to another point in time in one way only, by a completely determined series of intermediate points in time: from past to present to future.

3 Longevity and Entropy

We are aware of the life cycle of living things, from birth to maturity, senescence, and death. When you analyze the statistics of living and dying persons, you realize that the chance of dying are not the same for everyone. A newborn baby, a young child, a mature adult, and an old person all differ in the chances of dying.

For wolves, the last survivor dies at about age 15; for wild goats, all are dead at age 23; a thoroughbred mare lives longer, attaining age 30 [38]. Survival curves seem to look the same, no matter what species or object we are considering, even for rats, cockroaches, and automobiles. We know a dog does not live as long as a human; we know an elephant can live longer than a rabbit. So as we ask questions about how long we can expect to live, we must ask additional questions pertaining to how long one species will live when compared to another species. And we must discuss the expected lifespan for those who lead "normal" lives as compared to those who suffer premature death due to accidents. Obviously, animals in the wild are more vulnerable to early death than those in captivity. So there are many survival curves for each species, all with more or less the same shape but terminating at different age levels. Trees also age, though very slowly—much more slowly than living animals. So even trees are not immortal. All things die eventually, though the lifespan may vary.

Disorder or randomness is generally related to the definition of entropy. By material processes, the univers is thought to tend toward a uniform distribution of energy and hence toward a state of maximum entropy. This increasing entropy principle is one version of the second law of thermodynamics. Living systems accumulate negative entropy in parts of the structure; that is, they concentrate energy into ordered, highly organized states. This accumulation of negative entropy is not a violation of the second law of thermodynamics since other contiguous systems increase in entropy and the whole body still tends toward a state of maximum entropy.

The ability to decrease entropy is not a good general criterion for the identification of life, because many nonliving systems can do the same. However, the living system may be the only system that by natural processes concentrates energy and increases its own state of order. After the death of an organism, the membranes break down and the accumulated energy becomes randomly distributed in the environment. Usually much of the accumulated energy is not completely lost in death, but is utilized by other organisms, thus becoming part of a new negative entropy machine.

Since there is not yet a clear-cut definition of the living state, the best one can do is describe the major characteristics exhibited by known forms of life. Several characteristics are obvious: spontaneous movement, irritability, growth and reproduction, and use of nutrients. All stages of all living organisms do not show all traits; furthermore, some obvious nonliving objects are systems which exhibit, or seem to exhibit, some of these characteristics, though the mechanisms tend to be quite different from those in living systems. If one observes and examines organisms over long periods of time, several other functional characteristics are revealed, all of which are critical to both the short-term and long-term success of almost every type of living system. These include homeostasis, adaptability, mutability, evolution, and accumulation of negative entropy in some parts of the systems.

Homeothermic mammalian species differing greatly in temporal lifespan may have equal caloric lifespans: the total heat given off, measured over the lifespan, seems to indicate that animals generate approximately the same amount of heat [37], that *Homo sapiens* has about a fourfold greater lifetime accumulation and is an exception and the rate of living probably has a temperature coefficient comparable to that of other biochemical processes. This is seen as support for the hypothesis that aging depletes some sort of living substance that occurs as a consequence of physiochemical activities [86]. But some people say that the rate of aging is not simply a consequence of metabolic activity but of the more significant property of entropy production—and entropy production in highly evolved organisms such as vertebrates is governed by the size and capacity of the overall information and control system [86]. Thus we implicitly introduce the concept of the biological clock and attempt to develop the idea that perhaps there is a better way of measuring age, using some inherent, transitory physiologic variable rather than the usual measure of seconds, minutes, hours, and so on.

Some life-science researchers define an organizational entropy and show that [38]

$$Sorg = R(\ln u/\varrho) + \text{constant} \qquad (3.1)$$

where

$Sorg$ = organizational entropy
R = gas constant
ϱ = maturation rate for a definitive stage of development of the organism
u = mean metabolic rate for the same stage
u/ϱ = measure of the energy cost of carrying the development of an organism from one defined stage to another

A lower rate of entropy production permits the organism to live longer and do more metabolic work. The rate of aging and maturation are apparently related to the rate of entropy production of the whole system [64]: aging is related not only to how much metabolic work is performed but to how well the work is done, in entropic terms. Maximum entropy may correspond to death [86]. If the death of an organism is viewed as the state characterized by maximum entropy, we ought to determine the entropy production during the lifetime of an organism. Comparison of the total lifetime entropy production for different organisms should be enlightening, and from these figures perhaps some inferences can be made concerning life expectancy [38].

Hershey [37] defined an "organic entropy" for homeothermic systems as $\Delta S = \Delta Q / T$, where ΔQ is the basal heat per unit weight per unit time given off by the organism, T is the isothermal temperature, and ΔS is the organic entropy. He calculated the integral, organic entropy over the lifespan of various animals and found the calculated lifetime summation was of the same order of magnitude for the animals examined. Calloway [31] suggests that it is not the sum total of energy or entropy, but the approach to a lower critical level, which signals the onset of death. He puts this figure as 0.833 Kcal/Kg hr for various animal species and suggests perhaps that this represents a universal characteristic for living tissue.

The human body is a highly improbable and complex system of organs and tissues which involve about 60 trillion cells [31]. While the body has a natural mechanism for restoring cells and combinations of cells to their proper states and functions, the process never results in perfect restoration and alignment of all the cells that make up the body. Thus some imperfection always remains. At first these imperfections are unnoticeable on a macroscopic level; with time, however, more and more cells are not restored to their original configuration and position. These imperfections thus gradually accumulate until the critical level of imperfections occurs and the entire system collapses.

The aging process is always accompanied by the continuous development of imperfections. The lifespan of human beings depends on their environment, heredity, life style, nutrition, and mental state. Under certain conditions, a person may live over 100 years. From one point of view, the essential feature of living organisms is their ability to capture, transform, and store various forms of energy according to specific instructions carried by their individual genetic material. Living organisms need to acquire energy to do biological work for maintaining their life. Some biological work is easily understood. For example, the heart has to work as it pumps blood. Some biological work is less obvious: for example, the work done by the intestine in absorbing foodstuffs. Work is also done when there is a high level of genetic and nervous activity. To function effectively, biological systems must be programmed to acquire information about the internal and external environment. This type of work controls energetic processes, organizes biostructures, and controls the energy needed for fast response to stimuli.

Energy is useful when it can be converted into work. Entropy laws state there is always a certain amount of energy which changes into a "lower-quality" form and becomes less available to do work. This is not caused by an inherent problem of design in any particular engine or process; it is a law of the universe which applies, as far as we know, from the smallest atom to the largest galaxy.

Let us denote S as the entropy of the human system. We can write the following equation [65]:

$$S = \log g(N, E) \qquad (3.2)$$

where

N = number of particles in the human system
E = internal energy of the human system

The form of this equation tells us that entropy increases as the number of cells and the total energy within the body increases. Thus as the body grows beyond some sort of optimal configuration, more disorder occurs within it. Also as we eat, we increase our total energy content and more disorder again occurs.

From the many definitions of entropy related to disorder, probability of certain states of systems, presence of uncertainty, and topology, we can draw some inferences about the relationships between the entropy of a physical system and other physical quantities [41, 65].

1.   An increase in internal energy of a system increases its entropy.
2.   A system will decay faster if insufficient work from its surroundings is applied to the system or insufficient internal work is done inside the system.
3.   A soft system (as fats) deteriorates faster than a hard one (as muscles).
4.   An intake of molecules will increase the entropy of the system.
5.   The passage of time will cause the entropy of a system to increase automatically unless adequate negative entropy is supplied.
6.   As the entropy of a system increases, the degree of random activities within the system will increase as will the complexity of the system.
7.   As a system's entropy increases, its energy becomes less available for doing useful work.

Aging in biological systems is a consequence of the production of entropy concomitant with its metabolic activity [64]. Entropy is a physical quantity which governs how well the work is done in the system [9]. Samaras [65] applied the above ideas to human systems to get the following guidelines for increasing the lifespan of humans.

1. Keep food intake, especially carbohydrates, to a minimum, just enough to meet the needs of the body for internal and external work.
2. Internal work must be done by the body to maintain its configuration and prevent decay.
3. Hard or tough tissues, bones, and muscles deteriorate at a reduced rate.
4. Avoidance of fat and excessive muscular development, unless needed to do one's job, will extend life.

While the first law of thermodynamics states that energy can be converted into other forms of energy, the second law says that not all forms of energy are equivalent. The conversion from one type of energy into another depends on what the relative entropies of the two states are [42].

We cannot prevent the internal production of entropy inside our bodies [86]. However, the intake of foodstuffs of high-quality energy (such as free energy) will introduce negentropy into our body system [47]. We cannot avoid death [38]. However, we may expect to extend our lifespan if we reduce our generation of entropy by adding negentropy to our body systems through rest, sleep, food, and exercise. The degree of this slowdown depends on how much negentropy is added throughout our lifetime. Thus the job of extending our lifespan by adding negentropy requires us to know [55]

1. What kind of negentropic activities are best for keeping the body in optimum condition.
2. How much of these negentropic activities are needed for best results; how often and over what period.
3. How fast should one increase negentropic activities over one's lifetime.

Prigogine [49] and Georgescu-Roegen [28, 29] are both concerned with the second law of thermodynamics: Prigogine with his interest in nonequilibrium dissipative chemical and social structures, and Georgescu-Roegen in his analysis of economic systems. Prigogine stresses mathematical principles leading to the description of self-organization under conditions of change or fluctuation. He knew from biology that order and nonequilibrium phenomena were related. Increased complexity leading to increased order is virtually the definition of evolution. In other words, states were derived from nonequilibrium processes, driven toward another form of becoming. Prigogine was interested in the entropy aspects of new structures; one example, according to Prigogine, of a dissipative, nonequilibrium structure is a town, an open system, analogous to the living cell.

Georgescu-Roegen says the system of economic thought ignores entropy because of its blind faith in reversibility. He and John Allred [45, 46] have begun doing entropy analysis of systems and structures for maximizing efficiency of design and function. Georgescu-Roegen believes entropy is closely related to the economic process and adds important new perceptions to the marketing system. He and Allred say systems have been operating on the first law of thermodynamics conservation of energy and matter principles, rather than on entropy analysis. The second law of thermodynamics and its associated entropy concepts allow that energy, which may be conserved, is transformed and something is lost in the process (the availability for doing work). The second law implies that there cannot be unlimited substitution of technology and capital for resources. Georgescu-Roegen says the economic process consists solely of the transformation of states of low entropy to high entropy. Allred suggests extending Georgescu-Roegen's ideas into the realm of decision making (which involves information transport) and cash flow, amortization, and interest charges. Georgescu-Roegen proposes that the economic process is irreversible and makes a distinction between valuable resources (low entropy) and the final output of valueless waste (high entropy). He calls it a myth of the economic profession that resources are properly measured in economic not physical terms.

Since L. Boltzmann's time it has been customary to identify entropy as a measure of disorder and interpret the second law of thermodynamics as a principle of increasing disorder. Isolated systems as well as equilibrium systems which may exchange energy and matter with the surroundings attain a maximum disorder, subject to constraints such as constant temperature. In equilibrium systems there may appear structures (crystals, for example) which have extremes in one of the thermodynamic potentials. All equilibrium structures are stable to small perturbations. Since the turn of the century phenomena have been identified which seemed to operate differently. Among them were a periodic precipitation phenomenon where a concentrated salt solution such as lead nitrate diffuses into a lyophilic gel such as agar-agar containing potassium iodide. A precipitation of lead iodide forms discontinuous bands (Liesegang rings) parallel to the diffusion front. Other examples of systems initially far from equilibrium are the Belousoff-Zhabotinsky reaction (bromination of malonic acid) and Bernard cells (thermal stability in horizontal layers of a fluid which is heated from below, a cellular convection structure).

The departure from classical equilibrium thermodynamics started with Onsager in 1931. He analyzed nonequilibrium situations not too far from equilibrium by showing that linear relations hold for the association of fluxes (heat and matter) with thermodynamics forces (temperature and chemical potential). Onsager coined the expression "the principle of least dissipation of energy" which applied to stationary states in the linear region. This statement implies that a physical system open to fluxes evolves until it attains a stationary state where the rate of dissipation is minimal. Prigogine proved this implication in 1945 and called it the principle of minimum entropy production.

Prigogine and coworkers asserted that near-equilibrium stationary states with minimum entropy production are uninteresting (the entropy production term was a Lyapounov function implying that the stationary states are always stable). Thus any spontaneous fluctuation arising in this system regresses in time and disappears. Such a system near equilibrium cannot evolve spontaneously to new and interesting structures. Prigogine wrote that systems far from equilibrium with nonlinearities (autocatalytic or feedback loops) can evolve spontaneously to new structures. He refers to equilibrium or near-equilibrium states as the thermodynamic branch, whereas the new structures are called dissipative structures. Beyond the instability of the thermodynamic branch, physical systems show a new type of organization. The dissipative structures can be maintained only through a sufficient flow of energy and mattery. The work required to maintain the system far from equilibrium is the source of the formation of order. Fluctuations play a crucial role near the point of instability; they become large and are built up by the nonlinear behavior of the system into dissipative structures.

Glansdorf and Prigogine [30] in 1971 published a monograph on the theory of stability in the thermodynamic branch, where

$$\Delta S = \delta S + \tfrac{1}{2}\delta^2 S + \cdots,$$

and $\tfrac{1}{2}\delta^2 S$ is the excess entropy.

If $(\partial/\partial t)\delta^2 S > 0$, then the excess entropy is a Lyapounov function and the state is stable. A sufficient condition of instability is $(\partial/\partial t)\delta^2 S < 0$. This analysis is limited to small fluctuations since higher-order terms in the ΔS expansion have been neglected.

The possibility of building order through fluctuations under extreme nonequilibrium conditions has implications for biomorphology, embryology, and evolution. The ideas of self-organization are not limited to chemical and biological systems. Other applications are in fields such as population dynamics, meteorology, economics, and even the urban existence of a big city which can survive only as long as food, fuel, and so on flow in while wastes flow out.

In thermodynamics, the second law appears as the evolution law of continuous disorganization or the disappearance of structure introduced by the initial conditions. In biology or sociology, the idea of evolution is, on the contrary, related to the increase in organization, resulting in structure whose complexity is ever increased. Thus the classical thermodynamic point of view indicated that chaos is progressively taking over, whereas biology points in the opposite direction. Are there two sets of physical laws that need to be involved to account for such differences in behavior? Prigogine says there is only one type of physical law but different thermodynamic situations: near and far from equilibrium. Destruction of structure is the typical behavior in the neighborhood of thermodynamic equilibrium. Creation of structure may occur when nonlinear kinetic mechanisms operate beyond the stability limit of the thermodynamic branch. Despite the differences, all these various solutions obey the dicta of the second law of thermodynamics.

Prigogine's ideas may be summarized as follows [61].

1. Closed systems and linear systems, in general, close to equilibrium, evolve always to a disordered regime corresponding to a steady state which is stable with respect to all disturbances. Stability can be expressed in terms of a minimum entropy production principle.

2. Creation of structure may occur spontaneously in nonlinear open systems maintained beyond a critical distance from equilibrium. The system evolves to a new regime, an organized state (dissipative structure). These new structures are created and maintained by the dissipative entropy-producing processes inside the system.

3. Thermodynamic equilibrium may be characterized by the minimum of the Helmholtz free energy, $F = E - TS$, where E is the internal energy, T is the absolute temperature, and S is entropy. Positive time, the direction of time's arrow, is associated with the increase in entropy. Isolated or closed systems evolve to an equilibrium state characterized by the existence of a thermodynamic potential such as the Helmholtz or Gibbs free energy. These thermodynamic potentials and also entropy are, according to Prigogine, Lyapounov functions, which means they drive the system toward equilibrium in the face of small disturbances.

4. Entropy production $ds/dt = \Sigma_\varrho J_\varrho X_\varrho \geq 0$, in the neighborhood of equilibrium. This is also the basic formula of the macroscopic thermodynamics of irreversible processes. Here J_ϱ is defined as the rate or flux of the irreversible process (chemical reaction, heat flow, diffusion) and X_ϱ is the generalized force (affinity, gradient of temperature, gradient of chemical potential). Near equilibrium there results linear homogeneous relations between flows and forces (Fourier's law; Fick's law), $J_\varrho = \Sigma_\varrho L_{\varrho\varrho'} X_{\varrho'}$. Linear thermodynamics of irreversible processes is dominated by the Onsager reciprocal relationships $L_{\varrho\varrho'} = L_{\varrho'\varrho}$, where L denotes the transport coefficients and ϱ and ϱ' are the transport processes. A second principle valid near equilibrium is the theory of minimum entropy production for stationary steady states. This occurs in the linear range when boundary conditions prevent entropy production from becoming zero (thermodynamic equilibrium); rather the system settles down to a nonzero minimum level.

5. Closed equilibrium states are stable when corresponding to maximum entropy values. If perturbed, the entropy can be expressed [30] as $S = S_0 + \delta S + \frac{1}{2}\delta^2 S + \cdots$, where S_0 is the equilibrium entropy value. However, because the equilibrium state was at a maximum entropy value, δS vanishes and stability is given by the sign of the second-order $\delta^2 S$ term (a Lyapounov function which has a damping effect on the fluctuation).

6. Prigogine [61] gives a specific example to illustrate the behavior of chemical systems far from equilibrium. If the kinetics are as follows:

$$A \quad \rightarrow X$$

$$2X + Y \rightarrow 3X$$

$$B + X \ \rightarrow Y + D$$

$$X \quad \rightarrow E$$

then the rate of appearance of components X and Y is of the form

$$\frac{dX}{dt} = A + X^2 Y - BX - X$$

$$\frac{dY}{dt} = BX - X^2 Y$$

The stationary or steady-state solution is $X_0 = A$, $Y_0 = B$. Prigogine says the stationary state solution is unstable when $B > B_c = 1 + A^2$. Beyond the critical value B_c, we have a limit cycle; that is, any initial point X, Y tends to the same periodic trajectory. The chemical reaction leads to a coherent time behavior; it becomes a chemical clock.

With diffusion, the previous equations become

$$\frac{\partial X}{\partial t} = A + X^2 Y - BX - X + D_X \frac{\partial^2 X}{\partial r^2}$$

$$\frac{\partial Y}{\partial t} = BX - X^2 Y + D_Y \frac{\partial^2 Y}{\partial r^2}$$

where D_X, D_Y are diffusion coefficients. In addition to the limit cycle, we now have possibilities of nonuniform steady states or chemical waves.

7. Closed systems evolve toward an equilibrium state characterized by a zero entropy production rate and a maximum entropy content. Inanimate open systems not far from equilibrium are drawn toward a stationary or steady state where entropy production has achieved a minimum. These open systems in the stationary state continue to generate entropy linearly with

time. Living open systems such as the cell or the human body may not achieve a stationary state. It is not clear whether the living system is near or far from equilibrium. Instead of tending toward a stationary state, living systems may evolve toward death which may be characterized by the organism slipping below some critical level of entropy production. Below this critical level, the system simply cannot support life.

4 Lifespans of Animals

Determining lifespans of animals is difficult for obvious reasons. Certainly there will be differences between animals in their natural habitat compared to those in captivity. Questions can be raised about the comparability of life in a zoo and life in the wild. Diets vary, enemies are different, and mating habits and selection of mates are less comparable. Nevertheless some fairly authentic data have been collected, as can be seen in tables 4–1 to 4–3.

Everything dies eventually, though the lifespan varies. Humans at 85 years of age have only 10 percent of their cohorts with them; that is, only 10 percent of the original sample is still alive. For the thoroughbred horse, the 10 percent level is reached at age 27; for the laboratory mouse, the level is 1.5 to 3 years, depending on the strain of mouse [38]. For dogs, the survival curves show that the lifespan of large breeds is considerably shorter than that for smaller breeds. Some researchers have analyzed survival curves for mammals and dogs, coming up with empirical equations which relate lifespan to body weight [38].

For mammals

$$\log x = 0.636 \log z - 0.222 \log y + 1.035$$

where

x = lifespan, years
y = body weight, grams
z = brain weight, grams

For dogs

$$\log x = 0.60 \log z - 0.23 \log y + 0.99$$

For organisms subjected to a wide range of climatic conditions, individuals from colder locations seem to be longer-lived and slower-growing than those from warm places. For example, some mollusks which were placed in jars at 100 days of age lived for 125 more days at 23°C while at 7 to 20°C, the additional lifespan was 280 days [38]. In experiments with rotifers, lowering the temperature 10°C could prolong their lifespan about four times its normal expectancy. Cutting in half their food intake could extend life threefold [38].

Table 4–1
Lifespans of Some Mammals, Birds, Reptiles, Amphibians, Fish, and Invertebrates

Mammals

Indian elephant, max. 77, av. 24c
Horse, max. 62, av. 30 small, 20 large
African elephant, max. 57, av. 40c
Donkey (ass), max. 50, av. 40
Gorilla, max. 36, av. 26c
Blue whale, max. 36, av. 18w
Lion, max. 35, av. 15c, 10w
Dog, max. 34 spaniel, av. 13 large, 17 small
Capuchin monkey, max. 31, av. 9c
Grizzly bear, max. 31, av. 20c, 25w
Dolphin, max. 30, av. 25w
Shorthorn cattle, max. 30, av. 20
Sperm whale, max. 30, av. 24w
Rhesus monkey, max. 29, av. 15c
Giraffe, max. 28, av. 14c
Pig, max. 27, av. 16
House cat, max. 27, av. 15
Dogheaded baboon, max. 25, av. 11c
Zebu (Indian) cattle, max. 25, av. 11
Moose, max. 25, av. 15w
Fur seal, max. 25, av. 20w
Hyena, max. 24, av. 12c
Little brown bat, max. 23, av. 13w
Sea otter, max. 23, av. 13w
Wapiti (elk), max. 22, av. 14c
American bison, max. 22, av. 10c
Brown bear, max. 22, av. 14c

Hippopotamus, 49, av. 40c
Indian rhinoceros, max. 45, av. 40c
Chimpanzee, max. 39, av. 15c
Zebra, max. 38, av. 22c
Domestic sheep, max. 20, av. 15 small breeds, 10 large
Tiger, max. 20, av. 11c
Sea lion, max. 20, av. 13c
Big brown bat, max. 18
Gray wolf, max. 16, av. 9c
Mountain lion, max. 16, av. 6w
Pronghorn antelope, max. 15, av. 8c
White-tailed deer, max. 15, av. 8c
Fox squirrel, max. 15, av. 9w
Marmot, max. 14, av. 7w
Raccoon, max. 14, av. 4w
Lynx, max. 12, av. 6c
Dingo, max. 12, av. 4c
Prairie dog, max. 11, av. 8
Deer mouse, max. 8, av. 4c
Cottontail rabbit, max. 8, av. 2w
Opossum, max. 7, av. 3w
Guinea pig, max. 7, av. 2c
Flying squirrel, max. 6, av. 5c
Black rat, max. 4, av. 2w
White (laboratory) rat, max. 4, av. 3c
House mouse, max. 3, av. 15c
Shrew, max. 2, av. 1c, 1w

Fish

Sturgeon, max. 152w, av. 46
Halibut, max. 70
Eel, max. 55c, 15w
Carp (goldfish), max. 50w, 15c
Pacific salmon, max. 41w, av. 12w
Striped bass, max. 20w
Cod, max. 16w

Sunfish (pumpkinseed), max. 13
Perch, max. 12, av. 10w
Herring, max. 12w
Rainbow trout, max. 9w, 4c
Black bass, max. 8w
Sea lamprey, max. 7w
Sea horse, max. 6c, 2w
Guppy, max. 5c

Invertebrates

Sea anemone *Cereus,* max. 90c
Freshwater mussel, max. 80w
Queen termite *Nasuititermes,* max. 60w
Atlantic lobster, max. 50w
Beef tapeworm, max. 35
European crayfish, max. 30c
Blood fluke, max. 28
Sea scallop, max. 22w
American tarantula, max. 20c
Periwinkle, max. 20c, 5w

Mediterranean octopus, max. 12c
Hookworm *Necator,* max. 12
Commercial oyster, max. 12w
Razor clam, max. 12w
Earthworm *Allolobophora,* max. 10c
Large scarabaeid beetles, max. 10
Sea urchin, max. 8w
Queen honeybee, max. 7
Silverfish, max. 7w
Edible snail, max. 7c

Queen ant *Lasius*, max. 19c
17-year cicada, 17w
Sowbug *Porcellio,* max. 5c
Acorn barnacle, max. 5w
Slug *Limax,* max. 5c

House spider (female), max. 7c
Planarian flatworm, max. 7c
Giant snail *Achatina,* max. 6w
Squid *Loligo,* max. 4w
Chesapeake Bay blue crab, max. 3w
Bay scallop, max. 2w

Birds

Turkey vulture, max. 118w
Mute swan, max. 102c, av. 68c
Sulfur-crested cockatoo, max. 85c
African gray parrot, max. 73c
American crow, max. 69c
White pelican, max. 52w, av. 12w
Ostrich, max. 50c
Domestic duck, max. 47
Bald eagle, max. 44w
Herring gull, max. 44w, av. 19w
Amazona parrot, max. 39c
California condor, max. 36w
Domestic pigeon, max. 35c
Canada goose, max. 33w, av. 14w
Military macaw, max. 31c

Domestic duck, max. 31
Cardinal redbird, max. 30c
Domestic fowl, max. 30
Whooping swan, max. 30w
Arctic tern, max. 27w
Adelie penguin, max. 26w
Canary, max. 24c
Caribbean flamingo, max. 23c
Kiwi, max. 20w
Mallard duck, 20w, 19c
European starling, max. 16c, 8w
American robin, max. 13c, 12w
Barn swallow, max. 9w
Budgerigar, max. 8c
Nightingale, max. 7c
Rubythroat hummingbird, max. 5w

Reptiles (in captivity)

Galápagos tortoise, max. 150
American alligator, max. 56
Nile crocodile, max. 40
Gila monster, max. 25
Boa constrictor, max. 23
Reticulated python, max. 21
Snapping turtle, max. 20
Honduran caiman, max. 8

Texas rattlesnake, max. 16
Painted turtle, max. 11
Gopher tortoise, max. 8
Eastern garter snake, max. 6
Tree iguana, max. 5
Mediterranean chameleon, max. 4
Gecko, max. 4
European viper, max. 2

Amphibians (in captivity)

Giant salamander, max. 50
American toad, max. 36c, 15w
Spotted salamander, max. 24
Bullfrog, max. 16

Tree frog, max. 15
Mudpuppy, max. 9
Grassfrog, max. 6
Spotted newt, max. 3

Source: D. Hershey, *Lifespan and Factors Affecting It* (Springfield, Ill.: Charles C. Thomas, 1974).
max. = maximum on record, years; av. = average, years; c = in captivity; w = wild.

This type of information suggests that longevity correlations need to be qualified, bringing other parameters into the description. There are relationships between lifespan and diet, body-surface area, weight, and metabolic rate; and a dependence has even been found between brain size and lifespan. Birds live longer than mammals of comparable size. Cold-blooded animals live longer than birds or mammals, and it is suspected that these

Table 4-2
Lifespans of Trees

Bristlecone pine, max. 4600, rep. 30, ht. 50, diam. 7
Bigtree, max. 3000, rep. 60, ht. 272, diam. 32
Coastal redwood, max. 3000, rep. 20, ht. 368, diam. 21
Olive, max. 2000, rep. 4–8, ht. 50, diam. 3
Bald cypress, max. 1200, rep. 20, ht. 122, diam. 13
Douglas fir, max. 1000, rep. 20, ht. 221, diam. 17
Western red cedar, max. 800, rep. 15–25, ht. 250, diam. 20
Sitka spruce, max. 750, rep. 20, ht. 180, diam. 16
Sugar pine, max. 600, rep. 7, ht. 220, diam. 10
Western hemlock, max. 600, rep. 20–30, ht. 260, diam. 9
White oak, max. 600, rep. 20, ht. 100, diam. 8
Western yellow pine, max. 500, rep. 5–20, ht. 162, diam. 9
Eastern white pine, max. 500, rep. 10, ht. 120, diam 6
Sycamore, max. 500, rep. 25, ht. 120, diam. 14
Longleaf pine, max. 400, rep. 16–20, ht. 120, diam. 4
American beech, max. 400, rep. 40, ht. 100, diam. 4
Red oak, max. 400, rep. 25, ht. 70, diam. 11
White spruce, max. 350, rep. 10–15, ht. 120, diam. 4
Eastern red cedar, max. 300, rep. 10–15, ht. 100, diam. 4
Lodgepole pine, max. 300, rep. 5–20, ht. 150, diam. 3
Shagbark hickory, max. 300, rep. 40, ht. 122, diam. 4
White ash, max. 300, rep. 20, ht. 125, diam. 6
Sweet gum, max. 300, rep. 20–25, ht. 200, diam. 6
American elm, max. 300, rep. 15, ht. 160, diam. 11
Yellow poplar, max. 250, rep. 15–20, ht. 120, diam. 12
Tamarack, max. 200, rep. 20, ht. 100, diam. 3
Tea tree, max. 200, rep. 4, ht. 30, diam. 0.5
Saguaro cactus, max. 200, rep. 24, ht. 30, diam. 2
Balsam fir, max. 150, rep. 15, ht. 85, diam. 3
Basswood, max. 140, rep. 15, ht. 125, diam. 5
Flowering dogwood, max. 125, rep. 5, ht. 50, diam. 1.5
Honey locust, max. 120, rep. 10, ht. 140, diam. 6
Paper birch, max. 100, rep. 15, ht. 120, diam. 5
Quaking aspen, max. 100, rep. 5–20, ht. 120, diam. 4.5
Breadfruit, max. 100, rep. 8, ht. 100, diam. 3
Apple, max. 80, rep. 4, ht. 25, diam. 1
Cacao, max. 50, rep. 4, ht. 30, diam. 2
Coconut, max. 40, rep. 4–10, ht. 100, diam. 1

Source: D. Hershey, *Lifespan and Factors Affecting It* (Springfield, Ill.: Charles C. Thomas, 1974).

Max. = maximum recorded age, years; rep. = begin reproduction, years; ht. = tallest height, feet; diam. = diameter at 4½ feet above the ground at maximum size, feet.

cold-blooded creatures have a rate of aging that is sharply temperature dependent [38].

If I could hibernate and thus lower my metabolic rate, would I live longer? (A bat spends three-quarters of its life hibernating and lives to be 18 years old.) If I lower my temperature, will I lower my rate of living and thus live longer? Table 4–4 supports these ideas, as applied to the water flea.

Table 4–3
More Lifespan Data on Living Things

	Usual Length of Life	Maximum Life
Man	70–80	110?
Lion	20–25	40
Dog	10–12	34
Cow	20–25	30
Horse	40–50	62
Pigeon	50	—
Chicken	20	—
Alligator	—	40
Giant turtle	—	152
Catfish	—	80
Housefly	—	76 days
Fruit fly	—	37 days
Beetle	—	7–11 days
Spider	—	7
Sheep	10–15	20
Goat	12–15	19
Camel	25–45	50
Pig	16	27
Elephant	70	98
Owl	—	68
Goose	80	—
Salamander	—	11
Goldfish	—	6–7
Oyster	—	10
Queen bee	—	5
Ant (worker)	—	5
Earthworm	—	10

Source: D. Hershey, *Lifespan and Factors Affecting It* (Springfield, Ill.: Charles C. Thomas, 1974).

Table 4–4
Temperature Effects on Lifespan for the Water Flea

Temperature, °C	Lifespan
5	4.2
9	11.1
15	14.3
21	9.2
27	6.5
33	4.7

Source: D. Hershey, *Lifespan and Factors Affecting It* (Springfield, Ill.: Charles C. Thomas, 1974).

It is interesting to observe from the data in table 4–4 that there seems to be an optimum temperature for maximum lifespan of the water flea. Depart in either direction from this optimum and the lifespan is diminished significantly. For trout and the drosophila fly, raising the temperature of their milieu increases their metabolic rate and shortens their lives [38]. If I over-eat and am constantly well-fed, will my rate of living be higher than usual; and will I therefore live a shorter life than others? (Overfed houseflies are shorter lived than a control group which was fed normally [38].) Does it matter how long it takes me to reach full size; and if it does, can I alter my growth rate by control of my diet? (Small apes reach full size at age 3 and live to age 10, while the chimpanzee attains its maximum size at age 11 and lives to age 40.) The ratio of lifespan to age at full size is about 3 to 4 to 1 [38]. Slow the growth, lengthen the lifespan? If a woman is fertile, will she outlive others? (For roaches, higher-fertility females have shorter lives than virgin females who lived up to 50 percent longer [38].) Any lesson to be learned here? If there were something to be learned, would it be worth implementing? If we are crowded together, as we are in many cities, will we have a shorter lifespan? The answer is yes for the drosophila fly [38]. Is it true for us? If I live where the oxygen concentration in the air is low, can that affect my lifespan? Apparently yes for some flies where a pure oxygen environment speeds up the rate of living and shortens life. Does this infor-mation on flies apply to humans in their polluted air? The cynical answer is that the oxygen concentration in the polluted air probably will not be a major factor affecting our duration on earth—other pollutants in the air will probably do a better job of killing us.

Radiation exposure cuts our growth and weakens our bodies' reaction to injuries. In exposure experiments on animals, the results indicate that a single radiation dose of 1 roentgen is equivalent in humans to 5 to 10 days of extra age. The radiation also cause increased tumor generation, as if we were older than we really are, when measured by the calendar [38]. Neo-plasms, such as leukemia, show up earlier in irradiated mice. Genetic errors are more prevalent after radiation treatment: liver cells of mice show about twice the normal number of chromosome aberrations after a life-shortening dose. With radiation, lesions and degenerative diseases show up in small blood vessels and in the walls of the arterioles. Small arteries are thickened with connective tissue. Fibrous connective tissue is found around the walls of the capillaries [38]. Death from malignant cancer in childhood is about 40 percent higher than normal for children who were x-rayed during the last 3 months of fetal growth than for those who were not [38]. Radiation expo-sure in a pure oxygen environment is deadlier than in air or pure nitrogen. Radiation shortens life by seemingly accelerating the onset of decrepitude. One dies of old age at a young age. Some diseases simulate the effects of radiation, particularly a disease of children called progeria, a rare disease which transforms the young child into an old person in appearance, with baldness, skin wrinkling, and coronary disease. These unfortunate children live only about 8 years [38].

Low doses of x-radiation or γ-radiation are generally not as effective as high-dose rates in shortening the lifespan of animals [38]. This implies that the damage, presumably genetic, is a multihit effect; there is a repair process present which can reverse the damage caused by single hits [38]. Chromosome aberrations in liver cells of mice caused by irradiation (mutations in the somatic cells) are reversible [38]. Life shortening can be induced in adult drosophila flies which are resistant to low doses of radiation by feeding them some amino acids during the larval stage which cause damage similar to radiation damage [38].

So perhaps a clue to the aging enigma is to be found in the alteration of cells and deoxyribonucleic acid (DNA) by radiation. There are experimental facts which lead in this direction [38].

1. The lifespan of offspring from irradiated male mice may be shortened almost as much as that of their fathers.
2. The effect of a whole-body radiation dose of 120 roentgens on lifespan is the same whether the radiation exposure is one dose or divided into doses of 20 roentgens.
3. Immature, developing animals are more sensitive to radiation damage than are adult animals.
4. The lifespan of various species is inversely proportional to the mutation rate of the germ cells.

It is generally true that heavier animals or those with large brains tend to live longer. There are also relationships between body weight and metabolic rate (and hence between lifespan and metabolic rate). Those species which have high body weights have low metabolic rates (per gram of weight); thus we may infer in a cautious way that an animal with a low metabolic rate, will live longer. Elephants (heavy, with low metabolic rates) live longer than rats (light, with high metabolic rates).

If you raise the very legitimate question about correlating lifespan with brain weight—that it's not the actual weight that counts but the brain weight compared to the total body weight that is significant—you can generate data such as shown in table 4-5.

The trends of table 4-5 seem to suggest that brain weight divided by body weight is a rough predictor of lifespan, allowing for some anomalies such as the results for the crow and parrot. We are smugly reassured, at this stage, to note that humans have the highest relative brain size of all the animals listed. But in our search for more definitive ways of determining the expected lifespan, other available information seems to complicate matters. A mouse heart beats 520 to 570 times per minute. The expected lifespan of a mouse is on the order of 3 years, which yields over the lifetime of a mouse an expected 1 billion heartbeats (approximately). On the other hand, an ele-

Table 4–5
Lifespan as a Function of Brain Weight/Body Weight

	$\dfrac{\text{Brain Weight}}{\text{Body Weight}} + 100$	Maximum Lifespan, Years
Man	2.67–2.81	80–150
Elephant	1.24–1.34	90–100
Horse	0.43–0.57	45
Bear	0.36–0.50	50
Dog	0.34–0.51	15–20
Crow	0.114	50
Cat	0.29–0.34	20
Squirrel	0.16–0.20	6
Insect	0.06–0.18	6–10
Mouse	0.04	3
Parrot	0.15	100?
Heron	0.046	15

Source: D. Hershey, *Lifespan and Factors Affecting It* (Springfield, Ill.: Charles C. Thomas, 1974).

phant's heart beats only about 25 times per minute. Its average lifespan might be 80 years. If we do the same type of calculation as we did for the mouse, we see that over the expected lifetime of the elephant, it too will have about 1 billion heartbeats [38]. (In 1908 a theory was presented supporting the finite energy hypothesis. Calculations for total lifetime energy expenditure for horses, cows, guinea pigs, dogs, and cats yielded a figure of 29 to 55 million calories per pound weight of the animal. Humans, the exception, generated 363 million calories per pound [38].) But it has also been shown that by restricting the diet of immature rats (feeding them nutritious food, but small quantities), it was possible to slow their development, keeping them in a state of immaturity for 766 to 911 days. Longer than usual. Then if the caloric content of the diet was raised, the growth rate was accelerated and the rats matured normally. In the process, however, these special rats had their lives extended about 200 days beyond those who had normal diets [38]. Can life in general be lengthened this way? Perhaps. Did the number of heartbeats for the special rats exceed the 1 billion level expected for the rats with the normal diet? We don't know.

We don't understand much about the simple process of growth; there are some wide ranges of growth characteristics among living things. For example, can you make anything out of the fact that the pygmies of the Ituri Forest in Central Africa average a whopping 8.6 pounds at birth yet only grow to about six times their weight at maturity [38]? They are human beings, as we are, but this growth pattern is not our expected behavior. Some researchers have concentrated on studies of height and weight measurements and other variables as a function of age in an attempt to understand the aging process. There are all sorts of unusual empirical correlations which can be used a predictors of, for example, our final height [38]:

height, inches = 1.88 × length of the thigh bone, inches + 32

which is applicable for grown males. For girls and boys, equations which are good, on the average, for 90 percent of the population are:

girls' height, inches = 2 × height at 18 months, inches + ½
boys' height, inches = 2 × height at 2 years, inches + ½

We can analyze growth by measuring the height and weight of children. From these experiments it is known that early and late maturing girls have menarche at about the same mean weight, but late maturers are taller at menarche. Two other major events of adolescence are: the first spurt in weight gain and the maximum rate of weight gain also occur at invariant mean weights [38]. These results lead to speculation that a critical body weight may trigger some adolescent events. Or it may be that during maturation the parenchymal cells continue to grow and fill in the space supplied by the capillary bed until the rate of diffusion of one or more limiting nutrients (or the rate of removal of inhibitory products) prevents further growth [38]. We know that the secretion of the estrogen hormone stops female growth. But how? As we grow, we produce more cells; the cells that do not divide get larger. Maggots of the common housefly hatch from eggs with all their cells and generate no more. Their cells simply grow larger and larger with age, accumulate fat, and somehow, when enough fat has been stored, maggot cells cease to grow larger. Having attained this station in life, the maggot stops eating and suddenly a few of its cells begin to divide and differentiate to become wings, legs, eyes, and so on [38]. Human brain cells do not divide, but increase in size and number until we find at age 4 that 90 percent of the growth of the human brain has occurred. On the other hand, human white cells die in 4 days; red cells die in 4 months [38].

A rough rule of thumb for survival and growth states that lifespan is equal to eight times the age when reproduction is first possible [38]. In some cultures, people eat the reproductive parts of sacrificial animals in an effort to thwart the aging process, hoping for rejuvenation. Injections of the male hormone testosterone can affect the body very dramatically, but this is not true rejuvenation. Brain wave patterns are altered by testosterone injections, as is the chemistry of respiration and nutrition. The red cell count changes and so does muscle tone. But the effects are not lasting and are reversed when the hormone treatment is stopped. In some experiments, cysteine and folic acid were used for rejuvenating effects, but nothing permanent has yet been discovered [38]. Surely we will hear about it when the secret of the fountain of youth is unraveled. Despite the various treatments which are of some temporary help, we continue to age and suffer from skin thinning (glossy apparence of the skin, wrinkling, a decrease in elasticity, and increased pigmentation), hair loss (and graying and coarsening of the

Table 4–6
Some Lifespans for Males and Females of Some Species

	Male	*Female*
Fruit fly	31 days	33 days
Beetle	60 days	111 days
Spider	100 days	271 days
Rat	750 days	900 days

Source: D. Hershey, *Lifespan and Factors Affecting It* (Springfield, Ill.:
Charles C. Thomas, 1974).

Table 4–7
**Proportion of the Population 65 Years
or Older, U.S. 1880–1956**

Year	*Percent of Population*
1900	4.1
1930	5.4
1940	6.9
1950	8.2
1969	8.8
1975	9.4*

Source: D. Hershey, *Lifespan and Factors Affecting It* (Springfield, Ill.: Charles C. Thomas, 1974).
*estimated

texture), eye cataracts (and changes in lens flexibility), muscle loss (through atrophy), joints less flexible (and swollen), and brittle bones [38].

Some researchers point to the diverse lifespans of various species and say that aging is endogenous and is related to a growth inhibition process, which in turn is related to the time when our fixed adult size is attained. Is it clear to you why the maximum lifespan of the house spider should be 4 days while the longhorn beetle can live to 45 years, the Galapagos tortoise achieves a sensational 177 years of age whereas the swallow lives only 1 year, the rhesus monkey reaches age 29, a chimpanzee can live for 37 years, and the Indian elephant is good for 57 years [38]. Superimposed on these data is the fact that females live longer and have lower basal metabolism rates than males. Table 4–6 shows how much longer some females live. But are they luckier that they manage to survive for longer periods than their male counterparts? Are they healthy in their old age? Do females live longer because they are subject to different hormonal influences or is longer life related to the work they do?

The old folks have become an increasing problem for the young as fewer of us die from disease. Though our ultimate, maximum lifespan has not increased very much throughout history, life expectancy has nevertheless increased, as fewer babies die at childbirth and as infants. As diseases are eliminated as the cause of death, life expectancy will increase.

The percentage of the population which is 65 years and older has gradually increased, as illustrated by table 4-7, but note that a larger proportion of the older group is female, since females live longer than males. But women reach their final height sooner than men and they tend to gain weight more steadily into later life than men [38]. What does all this mean?

Much has been written on aging; both scientific and social aspects have been covered [38]. The data are there for those who can avail themselves of a good library. But the papers in the journals and the books, useful though they are, do not provide a focused look at the factors affecting lifespan and the parameters which measure lifespan. With this in mind, the following is a summary of the published information related to lifespan and factors affecting it.

Factors Affecting the Lifespan of Human Beings

Many factors which affect the rate of aging of human beings are known. Some are certainly hereditary, others environmental. Senescence probably reflects a complex interaction of hereditary and ecological influences. It is difficult to disentangle the respective roles of nature and nurture in such a highly complex organism as the human being. It is even more difficult to evaluate the action of a particular environmental parameter in a nonexperimental situation. Here lies the difference between the approach of the environmental physiologist in the laboratory and the ecologist in the field. The former attempts to keep constant all but one of the environmental variables under study; the latter is faced with a complex of ecological variables, some independent, others more or less obviously correlated. It is little wonder therefore that conclusions drawn from epidemiological surveys have to remain tentative until the experimental gerontologist is able to confirm or disprove them.

The first category of environmental factors includes all the physical and chemical components of the environment, whether natural or due to the unplanned effects of human activity. Important examples are climatic factors (temperature, humidity, and solar radiation), soil and water composition, altitude, various pollutants, and ionizing radiation [15]. Though a good deal of work has been done on their short-term effects, far less is known about their long-term effects.

The second category of environmental factors encompasses all the effects upon humans, whether direct or indirect, of the thousands of living organisms which share the various ecosystems of the world. The living environment exerts its influence upon the human organism mainly through nutrition, pathogenesis, and parasitism.

The paramount importance of nutritional factors upon development and aging processes is well known [15]. Briefly, the great differences in average daily rations between populations arise from (1) the uneven potentialities of artificial ecosystems to produce the kinds of foodstuffs necessary for an optimal functioning of the human organism; (2) the large differences in the efficiency of the various land-use techniques in different regions and at different levels of technological evolution; and (3) the cultural differences between groups, particularly in the traditional ways of selecting and processing favored foodstuffs.

Pathogens and parasites also influence the rate of human development and aging, more particularly in the low-income groups and in tropical countries. This is especially so in tropical Africa, the most disease-ridden area of the world. Until recently human populations were probably more limited by disease than by any other factor.

Parameters Measuring the Lifespan of Human Beings

To find the parameters which might measure the lifespan of human beings, we look for information about human physiological adaptability throughout the life sequence.

Human adaptive capacity can be thought of as the individual's ability to cope successfully with the stresses of life. Morphological, biochemical, physiological, and psychological processes singly or in combination make this coping response possible. Because their functioning waxes and wanes throughout the individual's life sequence, these processes bring about changes in adaptive capacity.

Eight physiological functions were described by Shock [69] and tabulated by Strehler [75]; namely, maximum breathing capacity, vital capacity, glomerular filtration rate, renal plasma flow, basal metabolic rate, conduction velocity of ulnar nerves, cardiac index, and intracellular water.

All values reported here were obtained from Bafitis [1] and expressed in the same units originally used by Shock and colleagues [7, 8, 19, 50, 51, 68]. The values obtained from the literature including Shock's papers were pooled, where possible, as weighted means and tabulated according to function, age, sample size, mean, standard deviation, coefficient of variation, and percent maximal capacity. Individual functional age peaks were set equal to 100 percent. Other age values were expressed as the relative percentage of the maximal functional capacity. A relatively good approximation of change in the organ functions with age was determined and graphed. Also the coefficient of variation (the ratio of standard deviation to mean) was plotted for each function, by age, and analyzed statistically (see figures 4-1 to 4-8).

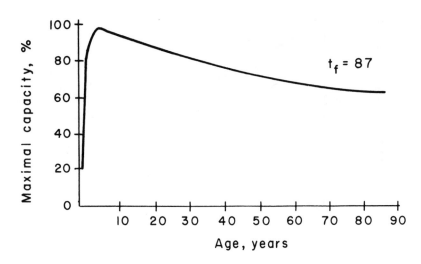

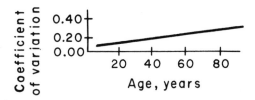

Source: H. Bafitis and F. Sargent, "Human Physiological Adaptability through the Life Sequence," *J. Gerontol.* 32, no. 4 (1977): 402–410.

Figure 4-1. Change in Glomerular Filtration Rate and Its Coefficient of Variation with Age

Seven of the eight measurable physiological functions rose from birth to peak or plateau between 1 and 20 years. Intracellular water, peaking about age 30, had the least quantifiable data between birth and age 30. If more data were available, especially between ages 10 and 25, the curves might have looked different for this measure. After age 30 these functions are generally considered excellent indexes of bodily health; all decayed systematically to what might be a critical level where the slope of the curve goes to zero. The ages where the slope is zero are 82, 87, 88, 89, 90, 92, and 95. The arithmetic average was 89. The significance of such critical levels with respect to expected lifespan will be discussed in chapter 6.

A very distinct rise with age was exhibited in the coefficient of variation

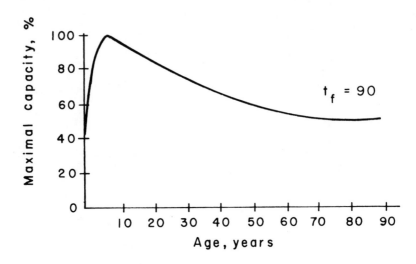

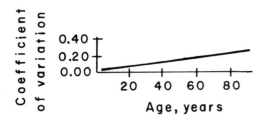

Source: H. Bafitis and F. Sargent, "Human Physiological Adaptability through the Life Sequence," *J. Gerontol.* 32, no. 4 (1977): 402–410.

Figure 4-2. Change in Renal Plasma Flow and Its Coefficient of Variation with Age

of all functions. This suggested that the range of individual variation becomes quite pronounced as one ages. This rise in variability with age for various functions obviously supports the idea of differential aging and adaptability, that is to say, with increasing age the functions of various organs and the general adaptability of the body system change with differing speeds in different individuals. This inference is supported by the fact that there is a statistically significant decline, from childhood to old age, in the correlation coefficients among biological functions dependent upon iron intake, metabolic processes involving fat and carbohydrate, and physiological processes in the oxygen transport system [15].

The finding that there is a chronological variation in functional capacity leads to the hypothesis that maximal performance of an organ is equiva-

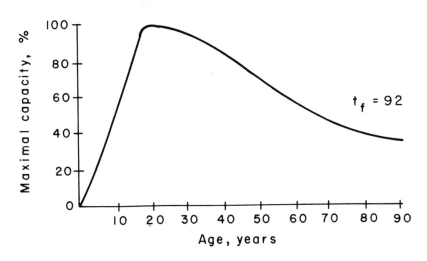

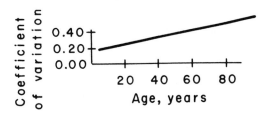

Source: H. Bafitis and F. Sargent, "Human Physiological Adaptability through the Life Sequence," *J. Gerontol.* 32, no. 4 (1977): 402–410.

Figure 4–3. Change in Maximal Breathing Capacity and Its Coefficient of Variation with Age

lent to maximal adaptive capacity. Adaptive capacity refers to the ability of the individual to cope with the events of life. The physiological component of this coping response ensures proper homeostatic function and control to the body. It should logically follow that as maximal adaptive capacity decreases the individual will subsequently become unable to withstand deleterious environmental influences and will suffer an increased probability of morbidity and death. Regardless of the general level of mortality and of major changes in the causes of death, the period of minimal mortality has consistently fallen between early childhood and about age 20. Both before and after this age span, mortality rises. Under Strehler's hypothesis [76], this period of minimum mortality is a period of maximal adaptive capacity. In other words, this relation suggests that as a consequence of the maturity

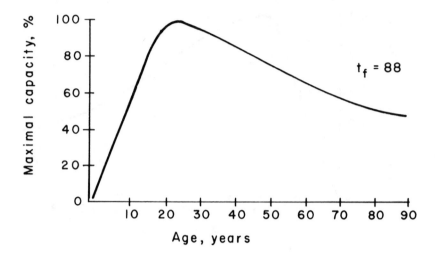

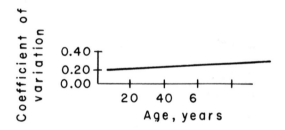

Source: H. Bafitis and F. Sargent, "Human Physiological Adaptability through the Life Sequence," *J. Gerontol.* 32, no. 4 (1977): 402–410.

Figure 4-4. Change in Vital Capacity and Its Coefficient of Variation with Age

and vitality of the functioning of important organs and systems, the ability to cope with insults is increased, which is another way of saying adaptive capacity is highest when death probability is at its lowest.

In recent years a seasonal variation in mortality in different age groups has been observed. In essence, there is considerable seasonal variation in the death rate in ages 0–4; little seasonality in ages 5–39; and in ages above 40, seasonality again increases. Kutschenreuter [44] postulated that an individual's tolerance of changes in weather decreases with increasing age on reaching age 25.

These results clearly lend further support to the concept of physiological function and adaptive capacity through life. The younger age group (5–19 years) is able to cope with seasonal variation in weather and does not

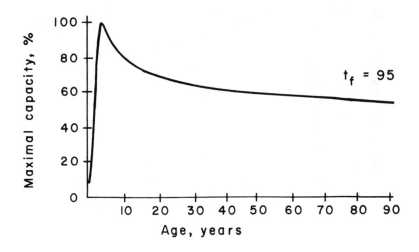

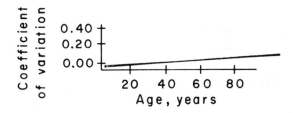

Source: H. Bafitis and F. Sargent, "Human Physiological Adaptability through the Life Sentence," *J. Gerontol.* 32, no. 4 (1977): 402–410.

Figure 4-5. Change in Basal Metabolic Rate and Its Coefficient of Variation with Age

exhibit seasonality. The very young and older persons cannot cope as well and thus show seasonal trends. This is consistent with the fact that there is poor, incompletely developed temperature control in the very young and impairment of control in older individuals.

It is well known that the age range for maximal athletic performance is in the early 20s for short-distance tasks and 25–30 in endurance events. This is consistent with our profile of adaptive capacity. Simonson [72] studied the effect of age on various types of performance and related physiological functions. He found that maximal oxygen uptake, which is the best reference level for aerobic work capacity, decreased with age. The speed of initial increase in oxygen consumed in work and oxidative recovery were delayed as one aged, and the mechanical efficiency remained unchanged or

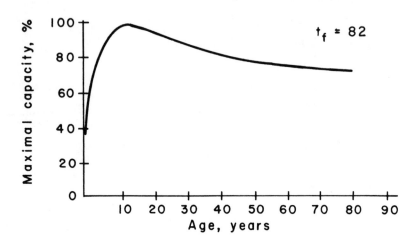

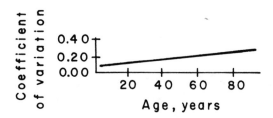

Source: H. Bafitis and F. Sargent, "Human Physiological Adaptability through the Life Sequence," *J. Gerontol.* 32, no. 4 (1977): 402–410.

Figure 4-6. Change in Ulnar Nerve Conduction Velocity and Its Coefficient of Variation with Age

moderately decreased in older age groups. He also found that respiratory efficiency, cardiac stroke volume, muscle strength and endurance (under moderately heavy work), all decreased with age, but endurance in static work remained unchanged with age. Pulse rate recovery was delayed and the speed of repeating movements by small muscles was slightly decreased, while motor coordination in small and larger muscles was unchanged and well maintained.

Terris [79] proposed that health could be redefined in functional as well as subjective terms. He urged the development of an epidemiology of health, using the measurement of performance capacity to provide a scientifically valid framework.

Although we know that adaptation is essential to human life, we still

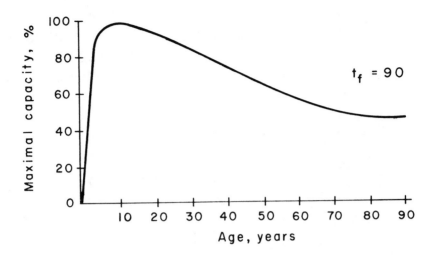

$t_f = 90$

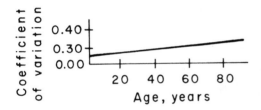

Source: H. Bafitis and F. Sargent, "Human Physiological Adaptability through the Life Sequence," *J. Gerontol.* 32, no. 4 (1977): 402–410.

Figure 4-7. Change in Cardiac Index and Its Coefficient of Variation with Age

cannot say that maximal functional capacity equates with maximal adaptive capacity. However, a greater understanding of adaptive capacity would expand the general scope of predicting the health status of people. A well-integrated epidemilogy of health then must include the concept of adaptive capacity throughout the life sequence. Our study provided an estimate of maximal functional capacity and found that the peak period is from 1 to 20 years of age for most indexes. It should be stressed that much more work is needed on this crucial period to arrive at a more precise set of normal values for the functions studied. The functions examined show promise of developing into essential diagnostic and prognostic indicators as well as important measures of adaptive capacity for an epidemiology of health study.

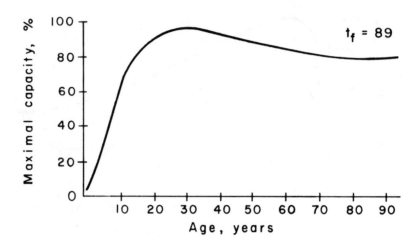

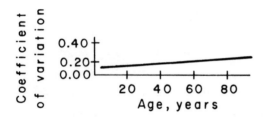

Source: H. Bafitis and F. Sargent, "Human Physiological Adaptability through the Life Sequence," *J. Gerontol.* 32, no. 4 (1977): 402–410.

Figure 4-8. Change in Intracellular Water and Its Coefficient of Variation with Age

5 Aging Mechanisms

Aging has concerned human beings since they first realized that it happens to them. They have attempted to avoid aging, reverse it, and, to some degree, to understand it. None of these efforts has thus far met with much success. By and large, aging is thought of in terms of the psychological, economic, social, and medical problems which it generates; it is thought of as being what it seems to create—especially what it seems to create in people.

Humans, as one kind of complicated living organism, suffer a gradual decline in functional potential with advancing age. This decline is essentially linear and is accompanied by an exponentially increasing probability of death [4]. These senescent changes are dramatically clear; however, little progress has been made in uncovering the causes for these changes which so distinctly mark senescence.

The notion that common effects arise from common causes, though intuitively derived, is one of the central tenets in gerontology. Clearly, neither this notion nor its converse is necessarily true, especially when applied to complex systems such as biological organisms. Yet in spite of its doubtful foundation in logic, this notion remains clearly implicit in much of the current thinking in gerontology and in the experimental work generated by this thinking. But as various levels of biological organization have been probed for possible causes of senescence, it has become increasingly difficult to discriminate among young, mature, and old. Although, with advancing age, organisms more frequently show signs of certain diseases, this increased incidence is the result of aging, not its cause.

Once a disease has occurred, however, it may contribute to the organism's loss of functional vigor. On the other hand, the deterioration of form and function, which are the hallmarks of senescence for an integrated biological system, seems to be reflected but slightly, if at all, in physical or chemical changes at lower levels of organization. Yet gerontologists, by what seems near-acclamation, have embraced the general hypothesis that organisms age because cells age. Many gerontologists also think that cellular aging is the consequence of molecular changes which occur in the biological information system; that is, the system by which DNA-based information is transcribed into ribonucleic acid (RNA) and ultimately translated into enzymic protein [15]. These changes are thought of as affecting a loss of information or information potential either because of random events occurring at the level of the genome or by the programmed expression of new and previously masked genetic information, deleterious to the system.

49

What makes this hypothetical construct so appealing is that it places the site of change in the genome, a biological common denominator, where changes can accumulate with time and can affect all manner of processes and functions throughout all levels of organization.

One of our objectives is to explain aging phenomena in terms of changes in the central biological information system. The physical and chemical changes in the information system which could deleteriously affect its capacity to efficiently furnish correct and timely information in quantities sufficient to sustain an organism's structural and functional integrity are potential areas to investigate.

To seek causes of aging we must understand aging mechanisms. Unfortunately aging mechanisms of humans and other mammals are poorly understood. To provide some order to the widely varied information on aging, we will study two classes of aging mechanisms: intrinsic and extrinsic. Intrinsic aging mechanisms mean that aging phenomena are regulated by inherent changes and are independent of other cells or extracellular factors. Extrinsic aging mechanisms mean that aging phenomena are regulated by alien changes, such as changes in hormones outside the cells or molecules in the extracellular matrix.

Intrinsic Aging Mechanisms

Intrinsic aging mechanisms are illustrated by Szilard's somatic mutation hypothesis [78], which proposes that somatic mutations accumulate to cause chromosomal inactivation and cell death; and by Orgel's error hypothesis [53, 54], which proposes that mutations in enzymes controlling genomic information flow, by reducing the fidelity of translation, could generate an exponential increase in errors, or an error catastrophe. Random somatic mutations are also proposed to account for the age-related increase of autoimmune changes, the consequences of which could include malignant diseases [10, 11, 12]. If intrinsic aging mechanisms predominate, the organism would consist of a mosaic of independently aging elements. The rate of aging in any cell might be governed, for example, by levels of DNA repair enzymes or by metabolites that quench free radicals. Recently, a correlation has been found between species longevity and DNA repair activity in fibroblasts [34]. Despite an emphasis on intrinsic aging mechanisms for nearly two decades, direct evidence for the accumulation of changes in DNA or polypeptide sequences is not impressive. The capacity of cerebellar neurons for repair of γ-radiation-induced breaks in DNA strands in senescent beagles [83] suggests that spontaneous mutations which may occur in stem cells or in nondividing cells are repaired throughout life.

Altered enzymes are found in some cells. An increase during senescence of inactive aldolase in mouse liver [26] is detected by immunoprecipitation. However, this phenomenon was not found in mouse liver lactic dehydrogenase [52]. Moreover, the cellular protein content and the activities of more than 80 percent of rodent liver and kidney enzymes remain unchanged throughout adult life [23]; this implies that the inactive molecules must be a minority of total cell proteins. The interesting inactive enzymes described by the Gershons [27] may originate from posttranscriptional modification or from genes activated during aging which code for immunologically related polypeptides with different enzyme specificity, for example, isoenzymes. No age differences were detected in the enzymatic properties of the active fraction of aldolase [27]. Further evidence against any general impairment of protein synthesis during aging in mammals is provided by the absence of changes in the composition of transfer-RNA nucleosides [40] or their chromatographic properties in senescent mice [24].

The possibility that mutation rate determines species longevity appears unlikely, though it cannot absolutely be excluded at present. A strong argument against a relationship between mutational load and longevity is that when young mice are given radiation sufficient to increase liver karyotypic abnormalities comparable to those of old mice, no effect on subsequent longevity was observed [16].

There is no correlation of species longevity in mammals with the amount of repeated or nonrepeated (unique) DNA sequences [17]. In addition, DNA sequence homologies and the number of copies of some repeated sequence classes do not correlate with longevity.

There is no evidence for any major or general loss of genes as is indicated by microspectrophotometric studies [77] or by DNA reassociation kinetics [17]. Studies of peripheral blood cell cultures of older humans show an increase of chromosomal abnormalities. Observations show that the capacity for hepatic regeneration, which may involve activation of genes silent since fetal hepatogenesis [14], is not lost during aging in rodents.

An increase of lipofuscins, or aging pigments, may be a type of intrinsic aging mechanism. These brownish, autofluorescent intracellular materials, which contain lipids and some hydrolytic enzymes [5, 71], increase in amount linearly with time and at characteristic rates in hepatocytes, myocardial cells, neurons, and other cells [80]. The rate of pigment accumulation may also vary with the lifespan of the animals, for example, accumulation per year in the human myocardium is one-fifth that in the dog [48]. It is unknown if aging pigments in all cells have the same origin and composition. There is no evidence that aging pigments cause defects in cell function, or induce lifespan-limiting phenomena in individual cells or in the organism.

The findings of Hayflick [36] that diploid fibroblasts have a limited lifespan in laboratory tests may also represent a type of intrinsic aging mechanism. The age of the donor is a factor: lung fibroblasts from fetal and neonatal humans undergo twice as many doublings in test tubes as do fibroblasts from adult donors [36].

The present evidence for intrinsic cellular aging in a living organism thus rests mainly on the results from transplantation of mouse mammary glands [18] and lymphocytes [84]. A possible alternative origin of these intrinsic changes is suggested by cellular phenomena of early development. Some cell types acquire a finite lifespan during differentiation. For example, in chick limb-bud morphogenesis certain cells predictably die, whereas their neighbors do not; selective cell death does not occur unless these cells made contact during earlier developmental stages with specific inducers of later cell death [66]. Since differentiated cells vary so widely in their proliferative capacity in life and in test tubes, it seems inappropriate to characterize loss of proliferation in certain cell lines as senescence of the same sort as that which is observed at the organismic level.

Extrinsic Aging Mechanisms

Extrinsic aging mechanisms are illustrated by endocrine and neural factors which regulate aging changes in target cells. For example, the atrophy of cells in the uterus, vagina, and other estrogen-dependent cell types is observed in women after menopause [35]; it may be attributed to estrogen loss [42]. Neural factors in cellular aging are demonstrated by the increased output of gonadotropin-releasing factors by hypothalamic neurons in post-reproductive women [67]; these releasing factors in turn increase the output of pituitary gonadotropins in women [81].

New methods of hormone assay have revealed age-related changes in the levels of hormones and in the activity of other endocrine glands [31]: for example, decrease in steroids produced by the adrenal cortex and gonads (pregnanediol, aldosterone, and dehydroepiandrosterone in humans [85]). Because many of the steroid hormones which change during aging also influence genomic transcription [33], additional cases of extrinsic regulations of the cellular genome during aging may be expected. Age-related changes in cell characteristics which are controlled by hormones, neural secretions, or other extrinsic factors may be considered as phenomena of cell differentiation.

The formal classes of extrinsic and intrinsic aging factors permit discussion of diverse age-related phenomena in a simple framework. Changes of cell-to-cell interactions, mediated by humoral or neural extrinsic factors, unquestionably underlie some major phenomena of aging. Yet it is unknown how many phenomena of cellular aging in life are the result of both intrinsic and extrinsic factors. Moreover, the presumed role of specific molecules in controlling aging should not be overextended, because some extrinsic age-related phenomena may be caused by entirely different processes.

The available evidence, though far from complete, indicates that the production of hormones and the levels of some receptors undergo many changes after maturation which cannot be the result of age-related diseases and which occur well before the premorbid involution. It seems extremely unlikely that these changes have resulted from intrinsic factors, acting independently at each cellular locus. On the contrary, it seems necessary to hypothesize that the changes of endocrine and neural loci during the various phases of adult life are interlinked and comprise a neural and endocrine cascade which is a mechanism of aging.

Aging Theories

There are many theories as to the cause of aging. This is so because investigators, as in other scientific fields, have tended to base their hypotheses on the interpretation of data obtained in their own areas of investigation and interest. That age changes occur in many different molecular systems can be described in both qualitative and quantitative terms. One of the main difficulties is the problem of assigning these changes as to cause or effect. As an example, the level of estrogens in females changes with age, but the primary reason is the alterations in the cells that cause these changes.

Theories on aging may be divided into three groups.

1. The very general theories, which, regardless of possible philosophic merit, do not offer much aid to those planning experiments or seeking therapies, such as depletion of irreplaceable matter due to the rate of living, a statistical normal distribution on the basis of undefined variables, converging of physiological variables to cause aging, the limiting value of undefined variables, accumulation of stresses and consequent stress damage, unfavorable ratio between the work output demands and the rate at which a system can function, and vitality and mortality concepts where vitality is defined as the maximum rate at which energy can be expended to restore its original condition.

2. The intermediate theories, which have a firm experimental basis and relate to one or more areas of the aging syndrome but rest on other primary chemical causes, include progressive cell death, cybernetics, hormonal imbalance, enzyme deterioration, autoimmunity reactions, somatic mutations, toxins formed in the digestive tract, reticulocytic effects, and free radicals.

3. The basic theories, which relate to causes that are as yet unverified experimentally, include the clinker hypothesis, protein hysteresis, thermal denaturation, and cross-linkage.

Some of the above theories had nothing more than casual observation to support them and some have relied on wishful thinking for support. Among them, only the wear-and-tear theory, the free radical theory, the cross-linkage theory, and the somatic mutation theory have gained more scientific evidence to support them. The wear-and-tear theory (the rate of living theory) states simply that the body has a programmed amount of energy or other property which is used up as a function of life and living. When we deplete the life substance, if the residual amount drops to some critical level or if the rate at which we consume it diminishes to some sensitive mark, we are sufficiently weakened and we die.

Food fuels the body as gasoline energizes the automobile. Restrict the food intake and you slow the rate of living and diminish wear and tear on the organism. The life cycle of invertebrates is lengthened by giving less food than that which produces maximum growth and development [38]. In an 1881 physiology text there is a reference to the dehydration of rotifers as a means of lengthening life [38]. Larvae and adults of species which show continuous cell multiplication respond to moderate dietary restrictions by lengthening their lifespan. Exceptions are animals which must draw on stored reserves in order to survive or those with a fixed number of cells and a need to replenish their reserves.

The lifespan of rats can be prolonged by restricting their growth through dietary means. After the restricted diet was replaced with a more normal diet, the survivors of these experiments resumed growth and lived longer than the control group. The effect seemed more dramatic in males. Similar results were found for mice and other rodents [38]. The basal metabolism of rats on restricted diets was intermediate between the normal young and normal adults. (An interesting question arises from these studies on rate of growth and ultimate lifespan: will the well-fed children in affluent countries achieve puberty sooner than less privileged children elsewhere and will this result in a shorter lifespan?)

Extending life by partial starvation is best done for very young rats: the normal lifespan of the white rat (500 to 700 days) can be extended to 1,000 to 1,400 days by keeping young rats underfed [38]. Tumors normally transplantable from one rat to another do not take in underfed rats [38]. When the life of an animal is extended by retarding its growth by dietary means, some parts of the body still appear to age at the regular rate. Bones become old and fragile normally, though they grow after the diet is normalized. Hair and skin manage to retain their youthful looks in the retarded animals; diseases come more slowly. But when the skin is cut, it seems tough—like older skin. Thus the bones of the retarded white rat at 1,400 days are fragile. Their eyes fail at the same rate as normal rats. The retarded animals never attain normal adult size, though they live longer than the control group. Optimal growth is not necessarily conducive to greatest longevity.

If an organ such as the kidney is severely damaged, it does not com-

pletely recover and hence becomes more vulnerable to disease ﹖
Damage in mammalian tissue usually leads to fibrosis which d
function. In our lifetime, as we suffer these upsets and accide
out. In some cases, increases in stress (disease) decrease life exr
Radiation is a nonspecific stress; mutagenic agents are another type oi stɩ௸௸
vector. For example, mice subjected to nitrogen mustard (a mutagen) and
typhoid toxin died at an accelerated rate. But the survivors lived as long as
the control group [38]. The same experimental procedure, but with x-rays as
the stress agent, showed that the survivors had a reduced lifespan. A tentative conclusion we can reach is that the mice able to survive the nitrogen
mustard treatment, the hardy ones, are essentially unchanged. This type of
stress apparently is not lasting. So in some cases wear and tear does cause
aging but there seem to be exceptions, such as shown by the nitrogen mustard experiments.

The rate of living theorists say simply that our body has a programmed
amount of energy, entropy, or other property which is used up as a function
of life and living. When we deplete this life substance, if the residual level
drops to some critical amount or if the rate at which we consume it drops to
some sensitive mark, we are sufficiently weakened and we die. (The engine
runs out of gas.) This model has some obvious validity for insects which
have no mouths in their adult forms and thus are limited in energy and lifespan to the stores of food they accumulated during their larval state.

In trying to find a rate of living explanation for the aging process, interest naturally turns to basal metabolism, which is the heat given off by the
whole organism under controlled, resting conditions. We have data which
show that the maximum rate of basal metabolism occurs during the first
decade of life, falls off rapidly during the second decade, and decreases
gradually thereafter [38]. Basal metabolism is related to oxygen consumption, and some investigators measure the oxygen used by the living system
and express it in terms of basal heat given off. We know that the greater the
metabolic rate, the shorter the lifespan; humans and mice both expend a
total of about 700 calories per gram of body weight in their lifetimes, but
mice use their energy about thirty times faster than humans and have a lifespan which is about one-thirtieth that of humans [38].

The free radical theory of aging proposes that free radicals are very dis-
ruptive to the body's biochemistry. They are present on the cellular level
where the aging sequence may be initiated. The net result of free radical
reactions with oxygen is new products neither usable nor desirable, perhaps
reacting with DNA and hence interfering with the coding of genetic material.

The cross-linkage theory (collagen theory) proponents say soluble collagen fibrils become insoluble and cross-linked with age and hence less per-
meable and stiffer. The passage of enzymes, metabolites, antibodies,

toxins, and other materials into and out of blood vessels and surface tissue is thereby diminished, and hence bodily functions become sluggish and prone to disease.

The somatic mutation theory (immunologic theory) of aging states that spontaneous mutations of somatic cells, propagated by cell divisions, cause the formation of inferior cells by changes in nucleic acid templates and further that mutated cells form more often in old individuals. The defenders of this theory note that older persons are more susceptible to cancer and auto-immune diseases, which may be caused by decreased activity of cells and diminished thymus function. Or it may be an altered condition of the anti-body surface.

Conclusion

Much of the research effort in gerontology at present goes into searching for basic molecular changes that are correlates of the observed senescence processes. This occurs because most fundamental biological research today is based on the paradigm that analysis of biological phenomena in molecular terms is the ultimate causal description. These molecular inactivations may indeed be causal in the sense of material causation, but even when they are proved, the knowledge will be of limited value, unless we also know those physical conditions that by their presence and magnitude, necessarily lead to the observed rates of molecular denaturation.

One fruitful avenue in the search for efficient causes is the comparative study of the characteristics that make a difference in the aging of different species (as shown by the existence of a correlation of the characteristics in question with differences in aging or longevity). Use of this procedure has established the existence of a limitation on mammalian longevity that is related to the rate and amount of metabolic activity. Sacher [64] observed that homeothermic mammalian species differing greatly in temporal life-span have roughly equal caloric lifespans, measured by lifespan energy expenditure. Also the rate of aging per calorie dissipated decreases as the size of the brain increases. Therefore Sacher suggested two hypotheses of aging.

1. Aging in biological systems is a consequence not of metabolic activity as such, but rather of the production of entropy concomitant with metabolic activity.
2. The principal factor governing the rate of entropy production in highly evolved organisms such as vertebrates and cephalopods is their size and functional capacity of the overall information and control systems.

From this point of view, aging can no longer be considered as simply a question of how much metabolic work is done; it is a function of how well the work is done, in thermodynamic and informational terms. This is one of our bases in measuring the rate of living of the human organism by entropic analysis.

6 Entropic Analysis of the Living Human System

The aging process has been studied for a long time, but no theory has been presented that provides all the answers to the "hows and whys" of aging. Since entropy seems to be one of the important variables in nature which may at times parallel the direction and irreversibility of time, the entropy concept appeals to many as a powerful tool in the understanding of the aging processes.

Entropy is a vital concept for our time. It has direct relevance in the study of shrinking resources, increased pollution, and greater sense of social responsibility, all of which characterize our present and shape our future [25]. It has been applied to various closed physiochemical systems for about 120 years. One form of the second law of classical thermodynamics is

$$dS/dt \geq 0 \qquad \text{(isolated systems)} \qquad (6.1)$$

which means the entropy of an isolated system never decreases.

The applicability of the entropy law to biological processes is a thorny problem in physical/biological reductionism. When the question was submitted to an international conference at the Collège de France in 1938, it excited much acrimonious debate, but no agreement could be reached [8]. The nub of the argument was that the second law of thermodynamics applies only to isolated systems: systems which exchange neither matter nor energy with their environment. Living systems, in contrast, must exchange matter and energy with the environment in order to survive.

Prigogine [57] formulated an extended form of the second law of thermodynamics which applies not only to isolated systems but also to open systems, that is, systems which exchange both matter and energy with the environment. Subsequently, Prigogine and colleagues [58] divided the total entropy variation into two parts: the entropy flow due to exchanges with the surroundings and the entropy production due to irreversible processes within the system. The internal entropy production is always zero or positive, but the external entropy flow can have any sign.

The living system is essentially an open system because it maintains itself by the exchange of matter and energy with the environment and by the continuous building up and breaking down of its components [3].

Processes cannot proceed in a reversible fashion if they have finite rates. The metabolic rates of a living organism (an open system) of necessity must not be too slow. Therefore the living organism contains a large number of irreversible processes [52].

Though it is conventional to speak of the living organism as being in "dynamic equilibrium," only in recent years has theoretical and experimental investigation of open systems and nonequilibrium irreversible processes begun. Recently [20, 21, 32, 58, 59, 60, 63] thermodynamicists organized a "thermodynamics of irreversible processes," part of which is developed here and applied to living systems.

We begin by presenting the second principle of thermodynamics. Let d_eS/dt designate the rate of entropy exchanged with the surroundings during time, dt, and d_iS/dt represent the rate of production of entropy within the system during the same time. For the total rate of variation in entropy of the system, dS/dt, we can write [53]

$$dS/dt = d_eS/dt + d_iS/dt \qquad (6.2)$$

The internal rate of production of entropy is related to the irreversible phenomena that occur within the living organism (chemical reactions, heat transfer, mass transfer, and so forth). The second principle of thermodynamics postulates that this internal rate of production of entropy is non-negative, that is

$$d_iS/dt = 0 \qquad \text{(reversible processes)} \qquad (6.3a)$$

$$d_iS/dt > 0 \qquad \text{(irreversible processes)} \qquad (6.3b)$$

In other words, irreversible processes create entropy. The external entropy flow rate, d_eS/dt, is related to the transfer of energy and matter in and out of the system. The sign of d_eS/dt varies and depends on the direction of exchange. As a result, dS/dt will be larger or smaller than zero depending on the importance of d_eS/dt. (It can be shown [57] that in a living organism, the rate of internal producton of entropy due to its metabolism surpasses by far that connected with other causes of irreversibility.)

For isolated systems (internal energy and volume are constant and no mass or heat is exchanged) we obtain

$$d_eS/dt = 0 \qquad \text{(isolated systems)} \qquad (6.4a)$$

$$dS/dt = d_iS/dt \geq 0 \qquad \text{(isolated systems)} \qquad (6.4b)$$

For a system with an internal chemical reaction of velocity, V, and affinity, A, there is a production of entropy per unit time which is expressed [58] by

$$d_iS/dt = AV/T \qquad (6.5a)$$

where T is the absolute temperature; and affinity, A, will be defined shortly. If there are several chemical reactions, the resulting production of entropy per unit of time is a summed contribution [58], that is

$$d_iS/dt = \sum_j A_j V_j / T \qquad (6.5b)$$

where the affinity, A_j, is given by

$$A_j = -\sum_k \nu_{kj} \mu_{kj} \qquad (6.5c)$$

ν_{kj} = stoichiometric coefficient of the jth chemical species in the kth chemical reaction

μ_{kj} = chemical potential of the jth chemical species in the kth chemical reaction

There has been interest in this concept of entropy production as applied to stationary states not in equilibrium. (In the stationary state the total rate of increase of entropy, dS/dt, is a minimum and may be zero [58].) This is possible when a balance is struck between internal production and external transfer of entropy with neither term being necessarily zero. Processes likely to demonstrate this are thermal diffusion and the Knudsen effect, among others [57]. For biological systems, one can often assume that a living organism is in a state approaching the stationary state [3], that is

$$(dS/dt)_{t_f} = 0 \qquad (6.6a)$$

where t_f is the time when the stationary state is achieved. For biological systems, the stationary state may be equivalent to senile death [3, 57].

Previous analyses [3, 57] of living systems from a thermodynamic point of view have led to these hypotheses.

1. In the course of living—and of evolution—there is and has been a tendency to modify the internal entropy production rate, d_iS/dt (the sum of metabolic processes), in such a way that

$$\frac{d}{dt}(d_iS/dt) \leq 0 \qquad (6.6b)$$

In other words, the rate of internal entropy production is continuously decreasing and may be tending toward a minimum.

2. The living organism may in the course of its life evolve toward a stationary state (senile death) which may correspond not only to $(dS/dt)_{t_f} = 0$ but also to a minimum of the total rate of change of entropy, that is

$$\frac{d}{dt}\,(dS/dt)_{t_f} = 0 \qquad\qquad (6.6c)$$

Let us again consider the human body as an open system. It is continuously exchanging mass and energy with its surroundings. There are many internal biochemical reactions, and therefore heat and mass transfer are occurring internally. All these processes are irreversible and interact with each other. We assume that the major source of internal entropy production is related to the chemical reactions inside the organism.

Again, let S designate the total entropy content of the human system, with $d_e S/dt$ representing the differential entropy rate of change with the surroundings due to heat and mass transport, and $d_i S/dt$ being the differential rate of internal entropy production (for internal biochemical reactions).

From the thermodynamics of irreversible processes [20, 32, 58, 63], we believe these relationships may apply to the human system:

$$dS/dt = d_e S/dt + d_i S/dt \qquad\qquad (6.7a)$$

$$d_i S/dt > 0 \qquad \text{(irreversible processes)} \qquad (6.7b)$$

$$d_i S/dt = \sum_j A_j V_j/T \qquad\qquad (6.7c)$$

$$(dS/dt)_{t_f} = 0 \qquad\qquad (6.7d)$$

$$\frac{d}{dt}(d_i S/dt) \le 0 \qquad\qquad (6.7e)$$

$$\frac{d}{dt}(dS/dt)_{t_f} = 0 \qquad\qquad (6.7f)$$

The chemical affinity, A_j, can be related to the Gibbs free energy, G [58], by

$$A = -(\partial G/\partial \xi_j) \qquad\qquad (6.8)$$

where

ξ_j = extent of the jth chemical reaction
T = absolute temperature

Using

$$G = H - TS \qquad\qquad (6.9)$$

and
$$(\partial H/\partial \xi_j) = -(r_j)_{T,P} \qquad (6.10)$$

where

$(r_j)_{T,P}$ = heat of reaction of the jth reaction at constant temperature and pressure

H = enthalpy

and by combining equations 6.8 through 6.10 we can obtain

$$
\begin{aligned}
A_j &= -(\partial H/\partial \xi_j)_{T,P} + T(\partial S/\partial \xi_j)_{T,P} \\
&= (r_j)_{T,P} + T(\partial S/\partial \xi_j)_{T,P}
\end{aligned}
\qquad (6.11)
$$

In textbooks on classical thermodynamics, it is shown that the term, $T(\partial S/\partial \xi_j)_{T,P}$, can often be neglected in comparison to $(r_j)_{T,P}$ [53]. We assume this for the living system. Thus from equations 6.7c and 6.11, we get

$$d_iS/dt \cong \frac{1}{T}\sum_j (r_j)_{T,P}\ V_j = -\frac{1}{T}(\partial Q/\partial t)_{T,P} \qquad (6.12)$$

where $(\partial Q/\partial t)_{T,P}$ is the rate of internal heat generation due to chemical reactions. By thermodynamics convention $\partial Q/\partial t$ will be negative. Thus the internal entropy production of a living homeothermic organism might be measured by its basal metabolism, as recorded by calorimetry.

Using the basal metabolic rate as the measure of our diurnally averaged energy or entropy expenditure has some drawbacks. Ideally, we would determine the heat generation over the full day and establish some sort of daily average. This is impractical under most circumstance. Thus we resort to the expedient of assuming that the daily, average metabolic rate, which drops significantly below the basal rate during the sleeping hours and rises above the basal rate during the day, can be characterized by the basal metabolic rate.

Energy Metabolism Measurement

An important advance in physiology was the demonstration that the amount of energy liberated by the catabolism of food in the body is the same as the amount liberated when food is burned outside the body [43]. The energy liberated by catabolic processes in the body appears as external work, heat, and energy storage, or

$$\text{energy output} = \text{external work} + \text{energy storage} + \text{heat} \qquad (6.13)$$

The amount of energy liberated per unit of time is called the metabolic rate. Essentially all the energy of isometric contractions appears as heat because little or no external work is done [31]. Energy is stored by forming energy-rich compounds. The amount of energy storage varies, but in fasting individuals it is zero or negative [9]. Therefore in an individual who is not moving (no external work) and has not eaten recently (no energy storage), essentially all the energy output appears as heat [43]. Thus in a resting, fasting state, the metabolic activity can be measured as the rate of heat transfer from the body to the environment. To make a comparison of the metabolic rate of different individuals and different species, metabolic rates are usually determined at as complete mental and physical rest as possible, in a room with a comfortable temperature, 12 to 14 hours after the last meal. The metabolic rate determined under these conditions is called the basal metabolic rate (BMR). Actually the rate is not truly basal; the metabolic rate during sleep is lower than the basal rate. What the term basal denotes is a set of widely known and accepted standard conditions, listed below [31].

1.   The subject has not been exercising for a period of 30 to 60 minutes prior to the measurement.
2.   The subject is in a state of absolute mental and physical rest, but awake (the sympathetic nervous system is not overactive).
3.   The subject must not have eaten anything during the last 12-to-14 hour period prior to the measurement. (Proteins need up to 12 to 14 hours to be completely metabolized.)
4.   The ambient air temperature must be comfortable, 62 to 87°F (which prevents stimulation of the sympathetic nervous system).
5.   The subject must have a normal body temperature of approximately 98.6°F.
6.   The pulse rate and respiration must be below 80 beats per minute and 25 cycles per minute, respectively.
7.   The subject should wear a loose-fitting gown to keep the same experimental conditions each time.

As discussed previously, for the human in a basal state, essentially all the energy output from the catabolism of food in the body appears as heat and the rate of internal production of entropy related to its metabolism surpasses by far that connected with other causes of irreversibility [57]. So we may calculate the internal entropy production rate by

$$d_i S / dt = BMR / T_B \qquad (6.14)$$

where BMR represents the basal metabolic rate of the human subjects (corrected for water evaporation from the skin and internal surfaces) and T_B denotes the constant body temperature of 309.8 K.

In principle, energy production in the living organism could be calculated by measuring the products of the energy-producing biological oxidations—carbon dioxide, water, and the end products of protein catabolism—or by measuring the oxygen consumed. These are indirect calorimetry methods. It is difficult to measure the end products, but measurement of oxygen consumption is relatively easy. (Since oxygen consumption keeps pace with immediate needs, the amount of oxygen consumed per unit of time is proportional to the energy liberated.)

One problem with using oxygen consumption as a measure of energy output is the fact that the amount of energy released per mol of oxygen consumed varies according to the type of material being oxidized. The average value for energy liberation per liter of oxygen consumed is 4.82 Kcal, and for many purposes this value is accurate enough [31]. More accurate measurements require data on the foods being oxidized. Such data can be obtained from an analysis of the respiratory quotient and the nitrogen excretion [31].

The respiratory quotient (RQ) is the ratio of the volume of carbon dioxide produced to the volume of oxygen consumed per unit of time. It can be calculated for reactions outside the body, for individual organs and tissues, and for the whole body. The RQ of carbohydrate is 1.00 and that of fat is about 0.70. This is because oxygen and hydrogen are present in carbohydrate in the same proportions as in water, whereas in various fats extra oxygen is necessary for the formation of water. For example:

$$C_6H_{12}O_6 + 6O_2 \rightarrow 6CO_2 + 6H_2O \tag{6.15a}$$
Glucose

$$C_{12}H_{22}O_{11} + 12O_2 \rightarrow 12CO_2 + 11H_2O \tag{6.15b}$$
Lactose

$$C_6H_{10}O_5 + 6O_2 \rightarrow 6CO_2 + 5H_2O \tag{6.15c}$$
Glycogen

are typical oxidation reactions of carbohydrates.

$$(C_{15}H_{31}COO)C_3H_5 + 27O_2 \rightarrow 19CO_2 + 18H_2O \tag{6.16a}$$
Glycerol tripalmitate

$$(C_{17}H_{33}COO)C_3H_5 + 29\tfrac{1}{2}O_2 \rightarrow 21CO_2 + 19H_2O \tag{6.16b}$$
Glycerol trioleate

are typical oxidation reactions of lipids [43]. Determining the RQ of protein in the body is a complex process, but an average value of 0.82 has been calculated [31]. RQs of some other important substances are glycerol (0.86), acetoacetic acid (1.00), pyruvic acid (1.20), and ethyl alcohol (0.67).

The approximate proportions of carbohydrate, protein, and fat being oxidized in the body at any given time can be calculated from the carbon dioxide expired, the oxygen inspired, and the urinary nitrogen excretion. However, the values calculated in this fashion are only approximations since the volume of carbon dioxide expired and the volume of oxygen inspired may vary with metabolism and respiration [31]. Therefore measuring basal metabolic heat given off by an oxygen consumption method can be inaccurate since it is based on a number of tenuous assumptions and uncertain data.

In determining the metabolic rate, oxygen consumption is usually measured with an oxygen-filled spirometer and a carbon dioxide absorbing system. Such a device is illustrated in figure 6-1. The spirometer bell is connected to a pen that writes on a rotating drum as the bell moves up and down. The slope of the line joining the ends of each of the spirometer excursions is proportional to the oxygen consumption. The amount of oxygen (in milliliters) consumed per unit of time is corrected to standard temperature and pressure, and then converted to energy production by multiplying by 4.82 Kcal/1 of oxygen consumed [2].

The energy released by test-tube combustion of foodstuffs can be measured directly by oxidizing the material in a bomb calorimeter (a metal vessel surrounded by water, all inside an insulated container). The food is ignited by an electric spark. The change in the temperature of the surrounding water is a measure of the calories produced. Measurements of the energy released by living organism combustion of compounds are much more complex, but large calorimeters have been constructed which can physically accommodate human beings. The heat produced by human bodies is measured by the change in temperature of the water circulating through the calorimeter, as shown in figure 6-2.

The caloric values of common foodstuffs, as measured in a bomb calorimeter, are 4.1 Kcal/gm of carbohydrate, 9.3 Kcal/gm of fat, and 5.3 Kcal/gm of protein [31]. In the body, similar values are obtained for carbohydrates and fats but the oxidation of protein is incomplete, the end products of protein catabolism being urea and related nitrogenous compounds in addition to carbon dioxide and water. Therefore the caloric value of protein in the body is an estimated 4.1 Kcal/gm [31].

Since in the basal state the metabolic rate can be measured by the rate of heat transfer from the body to the environment, we designed and constructed a whole-body calorimeter to measure the basal metabolic rate of elderly human subjects. The idea is to determine the rate of heat transfer from the body to the whole-body calorimeter. From the physical properties of the inlet and outlet airstreams, we can calculate this heat transfer rate based on previously established calibration constants and a heat balance on the whole-body calorimeter. The details are discussed in chapter 7.

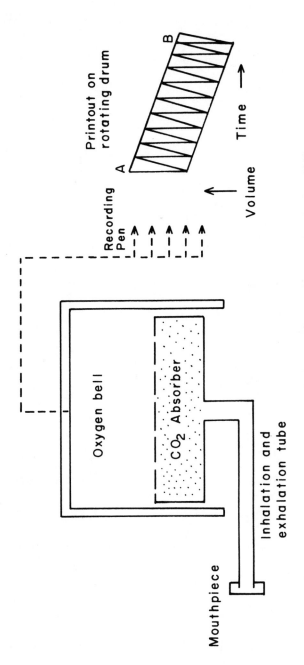

Source: Bell, Davidson, and Scarborough, *Textbook of Physiology and Biochemistry*, 7th ed. (Livingstone, 1968).
Note: The Benedict apparatus is a recording spirometer used for measuring human oxygen consumption. The slope of the line *AB* is proportional to the oxygen consumption.

Figure 6–1. Diagram of a Modified Benedict Apparatus, and Record Obtained with It

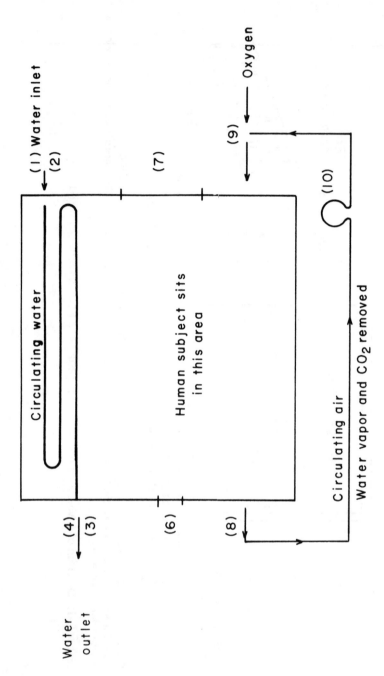

Source: Bell, Davidson, and Scarborough, *Textbook of Physiology and Biochemistry*, 7th ed. (Livingstone, 1968).

Note: Water flows from (1) to (4), and its temperature is measured at the inlet and the outlet. Air leaves at (8); water is removed from it by sulfuric acid, carbon dioxide is removed by soda lime, and oxygen is added at a measured rate; and the gas mixture reenters the chamber at (9). (2) is inlet thermometer; (3), outlet thermometer; (6), porthole; (7), window; (9), air inlet; (10), air cushion.

Figure 6–2. Diagram of Atwater-Benedict Respiration Calorimeter

External Entropy Flow Rate Calculation

To get dS/dt we need to obtain d_eS/dt (external entropy flow rate). We consider inspired and expired airstreams as ideal gas mixtures. From classical thermodynamics [73], we have

$$\Delta S_i, \text{mixing} = y_i \left[R \ln \frac{P_{i1}}{P_{i2}} + C_P \ln \frac{T2}{T1} \right] \tag{6.17}$$

where

ΔS_i, mixing = amount of entropy change during mixing from state 1 to state 2 for component i
P_{i1} = partial pressure of component i in state 1
P_{i2} = partial pressure of component i in state 2
$T1$ = temperature of the mixture in state 1
$T2$ = temperature of the mixture in state 2
C_P = heat capacity of gas mixture at constant pressure
y_i = mole fraction of component i in the gas mixture

For ideal gas mixtures, we have

$$P_{i1} = \pi \tag{6.18a}$$

(this state has only one component before mixing) and

$$P_{i2} = y_i \pi \tag{6.18b}$$

where

π = barometric pressure

If

$$T1 = T2 \tag{6-19}$$

then we can obtain.

$$\Delta S_i, \text{mixing} = - Ry_i \ln y_i \tag{6-20}$$

by substituting equations 6.18a, 6.18b, and 6.19 into 6.17. Thus we get

$$Sm = \sum_i y_i S_i - R \sum_i y_i \ln y_i \tag{6-21}$$

where

Sm = molar entropy of the the ideal gas mixture
S_i = molar entropy of component i
R = gas constant

For human subjects, resting (in the basal state) in the whole-body calorimeter, the interaction with the environment is mostly through respiration [43]. Thus we can obtain

$$d_e S/dt = \frac{\dot{V}}{24.45} (Sm^{(i)} - Sm^{(e)}) \qquad (6\text{-}22)$$

where

$Sm^{(i)}$ = molar entropy of the inspired airstream, 25°C, 1 atm
$Sm^{(e)}$ = molar entropy of the expired airstream, 36.8°C, 1 atm
$\dot{V}$ = volumetric flow rate of the inspired and expired air, 1/min at 25°C and 1 atm
24.45 = molar volume, liters at 25°C, 1 atm

From respiration data [22] we can get the volumetric flow rate and composition at standard temperature and pressure of the inspired and expired airstreams for human males and females. We compile these data in tables 6-1, 6-2, and 6-3.

Using the data of tables 6-2 and 6-3 substituted into equation 6.21, we can obtain $Sm^{(i)}$ and $Sm^{(e)}$. From table 6-1, we can obtain $\dot{V}$. Substituting $\dot{V}$, $Sm^{(i)}$, and $Sm^{(e)}$ into equation 6.22, we can get $d_e S/dt$ for human males and females. The results are shown in table 6-4 and figures 6-3 and 6-4.

One typical calculation of $d_e S/dt$ for human males age 16 is shown below. From table 6-2, we can get

$y^{(i)}_{O_2}$ = 0.2079 $\qquad\qquad$ $y^{(i)}_{CO_2}$ = 0.0004

$y^{(i)}_{N_2}$ = 0.7482 $\qquad\qquad$ $y^{(i)}_{H_2O}$ = 0.0075

$S^{(i)}_{O_2}$ = 49.0528 cal/mol °K $\qquad$ $S^{(i)}_{CO_2}$ = 51.0884 cal/mol °K

$S^{(i)}_{N_2}$ = 45.7744 cal/mol °K $\qquad$ $S^{(i)}_{H_2O}$ = 36.7974 cal/mol °K

Therefore from equation 6.21 we get

$$Sm^{(i)} = \sum_j y^{(i)}_j S^{(i)}_j - R \sum_j y^{(i)}_j \ln y^{(i)}_j$$

$$= 46.391 + 1.107 = 47.498 \text{ cal/mol °K**}$$

Table 6-1
Volumetric Airflow Rates during Respiration at Standard Conditions for Human Males and Females

Age	Male	Female
t, Years	$\dot{V}$, l/min	$\dot{V}$, l/min
Premature	1.34	1.34
Newborn	1.21	1.21
5- 7	8.93	8.93
8-13	7.37	7.37
13-15	8.12	6.86
16-19	7.15	6.03
20-29	6.37	5.38
30-39	6.89	5.82
40-49	7.58	6.40
50-59	7.27	6.14
60-69	7.02	5.93
70-79	6.12	5.19
80-89	5.22	4.45

Source: H. Faseb, "Respiration and Circulation," Federation of American Societies for Experimental Biology (Bethesda, 1971).

Note: Standard conditions = 25°C and 1 atm.

Table 6-2
Inspired Airstream Composition and Molar Entropy of Human Males and Females

Components	Mole Fraction $y_i^{(i)}$	Molar Entropy $S_i^{(i)}$, cal/mol°K
O_2	0.2079	49.0528
CO_2	0.0004	51.0884
N_2	0.7482	45.7744
H_2O	0.0075	36.7974

Sources: R.E. Bolz and G.L. Tuve, *Handbook of Tables for Applied Engineering and Science,* 2nd ed. (Cleveland, CRC, 1976); and H. Faseb, "Respiration and Circulation," Federation of American Societies for Experimental Biology (Bethesda, 1971).

From table 6-3, we can get

$$y_{O_2}^{(e)} = 0.1526 \qquad y_{CO_2}^{(e)} = 0.0422$$

$$y_{N2}^{(e)} = 0.7434 \qquad y_{H_2O}^{(e)} = 0.0618$$

$$S_{O_2}^{(e)} = 49.2352 \text{ cal/mol °K} \qquad S_{CO_2}^{(e)} = 51.3832 \text{ cal/mol °K}$$

$$S_{N_2}^{(e)} = 45.9536 \text{ cal/mol °K} \qquad S_{H_2O}^{(e)} = 35.712 \text{ cal/mol °K}$$

Table 6–3

Expired Airstream Composition and Molar Entropy of Human Males and Females

Components	Mole Fraction $y_i^{(e)}$	Molar Entropy $S_i^{(e)}$, cal/mol °K
O_2	0.1526	49.2352
CO_2	0.0422	51.3832
N_2	0.7434	45.9536
H_2O	0.0618	35.7120

Sources: R.E. Bolz and G.L. Tuve, *Handbook of Tables for Applied Engineering and Science,* 2nd ed. (Cleveland: CRC, 1976); and H. Faseb, "Respiration and Circulation," Federation of American Societies for Experimental Biology (Bethesda, 1971).

Note: The expired airstream is considered as an ideal gas mixture at 36.8°C and 1 atm.

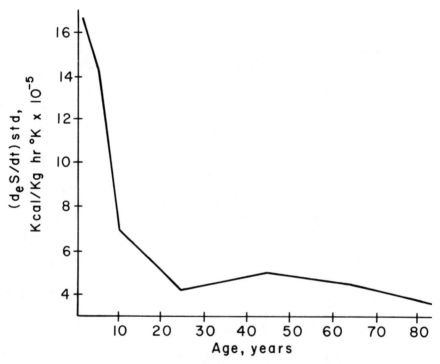

Figure 6–3. Plot of Rate of Change of Entropy of Human Males Due to Exchange of Entropy with Surroundings versus Age

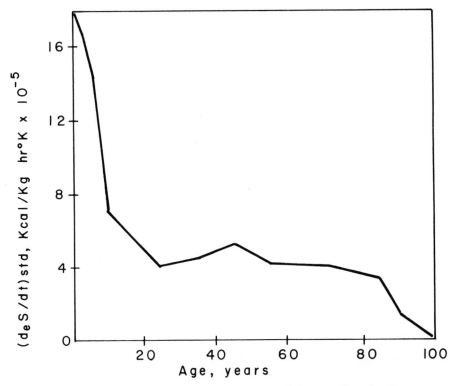

Figure 6–4. Plot of Rate of Change of Entropy of Human Females Due to Exchange of Entropy with Surroundings versus Age

Table 6–4
Rate of Change of Entropy Exchange with Surroundings (d_eS/dt), for Human Males and Females

Age Years	d_eS/dt, Kcal/°K hr Male	d_eS/dt, Kcal/°K hr Female
Premature	− 5.5279E−4 [a]	− 5.5279E−4
Newborn	− 4.9916E−4	− 4.9916E−4
5– 7	−36.8389E−4	−36.8389E−4
8–13	−30.4035E−4	−30.4035E−4
13–15	−33.4974E−4	−28.2996E−4
16–19	−29.4959E−4	−24.8756E−4
20–29	−26.2782E−4	−22.1941E−4
30–39	−28.4233E−4	−24.0093E−4
40–49	−31.2698E−4	−26.4019E−4
50–59	−29.9909E−4	−25.3293E−4
60–69	−28.9596E−4	−24.4630E−4
70–79	−25.3468E−4	−21.4103E−4
80–89	−21.5341E−4	−18.3576E−4

[a] E−4 is 10^{-4}.

Thus from equation 6.21 we get

$$Sm^{(e)} = \sum_j y_j^{(e)} S_j^{(e)} - R\sum_j y_j^{(e)} \ln y_j^{(e)}$$

$$= 46.051 + 1.615 = 46.666 \text{ cal/mol } °K$$

From table 6-1, we get

$$\dot{V} = 7.15 \text{ l/min}$$

So from equation 6-22, we get

$$d_e S/dt = \frac{\dot{V} \text{ l/min}}{24.45 \text{ l/mol}} (Sm^{(i)} - Sm^{(e)})$$

$$= \frac{7.15 \text{ l/min}}{24.45 \text{ l/mol}} (47.498 - 46.666)$$

$$= -0.04916 \text{ cal/min } °K$$

$$= -29.496\text{E-4 Kcal/hr}°K$$

Rate of Change of Entropy from Pooled Data

We used the basal metabolic rate data of Shock [70], Robertson and Reid [31], Boothby [31], Aub and Du Bois [31], and Fleish [31]. With equation 6.14 we can calculate $d_i S/dt$ from these BMR data. We determined $d_e S/dt$ previously, as shown in table 6-4. Thus based on equation 6.2, dS/dt can be obtained. The results are compiled in table 6-5 through 6-12. Sample calculation are shown in appendix A.

Table 6-5
Standard Values of Basal Metabolic Rate, (BMR)std, Internal Entropy Production Rate, $(d_i S/dt)$std, External Entropy Flow Rate, $(d_e S/dt)$std, and Total Rate of Change of Entropy, (dS/dt)std, for Human Males, Based on Shock's Basal Metabolic Rate Data

Chronological Age Years	(BMR)std Kcal/Kg hr	$(d_i S/dt)$std Kcal/Kg hr°K	$(d_e S/dt)$std Kcal/Kg hr°K	(dS/dt)std Kcal/Kg hr°K
25	1.0050	3.2440E-3	-0.0427E-3	3.2013E-3
26	0.9969	3.2180E-3	-0.0431E-3	3.1749E-3
27	0.9889	3.1920E-3	-0.0435E-3	3.1485E-3
28	0.9808	3.1660E-3	-0.0439E-3	3.1221E-3
29	0.9727	3.1398E-3	-0.0441E-3	3.0957E-3

Chronological Age Years	(BMR) Kcal/Kg hr	$(d_iS/dt)std$ Kcal/Kg hr °K	$(d_eS/dt)std$ Kcal/Kg hr °K	$(dS/dt)std$ Kcal/Kg hr °Kg
30	0.9646	3.1136E-3	−0.0443E-3	3.0693E-3
31	0.9565	3.0876E-3	−0.0447E-3	3.0429E-3
32	0.9485	3.0615E-3	−0.0451E-3	3.0164E-3
33	0.9404	3.0355E-3	−0.0455E-3	2.9900E-3
34	0.9323	3.0093E-3	−0.0457E-3	2.9636E-3
35	0.9241	2.9830E-3	−0.0458E-3	2.9372E-3
36	0.9185	2.9648E-3	−0.0464E-3	2.9184E-3
37	0.9128	2.9465E-3	−0.0469E-3	2.8996E-3
38	0.9072	2.9282E-3	−0.0475E-3	2.8807E-3
39	0.9014	2.9097E-3	−0.0478E-3	2.8619E-3
40	0.8957	2.8911E-3	−0.0480E-3	2.8431E-3
41	0.8900	2.8729E-3	−0.0486E-3	2.8243E-3
42	0.8843	2.8545E-3	−0.0491E-3	2.8054E-3
43	0.8787	2.8362E-3	−0.0496E-3	2.7866E-3
44	0.8729	2.8176E-3	−0.0499E-3	2.7677E-3
45	0.8671	2.7990E-3	−0.0501E-3	2.7489E-3
46	0.8661	2.7957E-3	−0.0498E-3	2.7459E-3
47	0.8651	2.7923E-3	−0.0495E-3	2.7428E-3
48	0.8640	2.7890E-3	−0.0492E-3	2.7398E-3
49	0.8630	2.7857E-3	−0.0490E-3	2.7367E-3
50	0.8620	2.7825E-3	−0.0488E-3	2.7337E-3
51	0.8610	2.7792E-3	−0.0485E-3	2.7307E-3
52	0.8600	2.7760E-3	−0.0484E-3	2.7276E-3
53	0.8590	2.7728E-3	−0.0482E-3	2.7246E-3
54	0.8580	2.7694E-3	−0.0479E-3	2.7215E-3
55	0.8569	2.7660E-3	−0.0475E-3	2.7185E-3
56	0.8547	2.7589E-3	−0.0473E-3	2.7116E-3
57	0.8526	2.7520E-3	−0.0472E-3	2.7048E-3
58	0.8504	2.7449E-3	−0.0470E-3	2.6979E-3
59	0.8482	2.7378E-3	−0.0467E-3	2.6911E-3
60	0.8459	2.7306E-3	−0.0464E-3	2.6842E-3
61	0.8437	2.7234E-3	−0.0461E-3	2.6773E-3
62	0.8415	2.7164E-3	−0.0460E-3	2.6704E-3
63	0.8394	2.7094E-3	−0.0458E-3	2.6636E-3
64	0.8371	2.7022E-3	−0.0455E-3	2.6567E-3
65	0.8349	2.6950E-3	−0.0452E-3	2.6498E-3
66	0.8335	2.6903E-3	−0.0445E-3	2.6458E-3
67	0.8321	2.6860E-3	−0.0442E-3	2.6418E-3
68	0.8308	2.6816E-3	−0.0438E-3	2.6378E-3
69	0.8293	2.6768E-3	−0.0431E-3	2.6337E-3
70	0.8278	2.6721E-3	−0.0424E-3	2.6297E-3
71	0.8257	2.6653E-3	−0.0417E-3	2.6236E-3
72	0.8237	2.6589E-3	−0.0414E-3	2.6175E-3
73	0.8224	2.6545E-3	−0.0410E-3	2.6135E-3
74	0.8214	2.6515E-3	−0.0403E-3	2.6112E-3
75	0.8207	2.6490E-3	−0.0395E-3	2.6095E-3

Source: Shock, N.W. et al., "Age Differences in the Water Content of the Body Related to Basal Oxygen Consumption in Males," *J. Gerontol.* 18(1963): 1.

Table 6–6

Standard Values of Basal Metabolic Rate, (BMR)std, Internal Entropy Production Rate, (d_iS/dt)std, External Entropy Flow Rate, (d_eS/dt)std, and Total Rate of Change of Entropy, (dS/dt)std, for Human Males, Based on Robertson and Reid's Basal Metabolic Rate Data

Chronological Age, Years	(BMR)std Kcal/Kg hr	(d_iS/dt)std Kcal/Kg hr °K	(d_eS/dt)std Kcal/Kg hr °K	(dS/dt)std Kcal/Kg hr °K
6	1.7849	5.7615E-3	−0.1316E-3	5.6299E-3
7	1.6687	5.3864E-3	−0.1160E-3	5.2704E-3
8	1.5525	5.0112E-3	−0.1004E-3	4.9108E-3
9	1.4363	4.6361E-3	−0.0848E-3	4.5513E-3
10	1.3200	4.2608E-3	−0.0691E-3	4.1917E-3
11	1.2706	4.1013E-3	−0.0681E-3	4.0332E-3
12	1.2211	3.9416E-3	−0.0670E-3	3.8746E-3
13	1.1717	3.7820E-3	−0.0659E-3	3.7161E-3
14	1.1222	3.6223E-3	−0.0648E-3	3.5575E-3
15	1.0978	3.5437E-3	−0.0618E-3	3.4819E-3
16	1.0735	3.4651E-3	−0.0588E-3	3.4063E-3
17	1.0416	3.3621E-3	−0.0558E-3	3.3063E-3
18	1.0247	3.3077E-3	−0.0527E-3	3.3550E-3
19	1.0088	3.2564E-3	−0.0515E-3	3.2049E-3
20	0.9933	3.2062E-3	−0.0502E-3	3.1560E-3
21	0.9851	3.1798E-3	−0.0490E-3	3.1308E-3
22	0.9769	3.1533E-3	−0.0477E-3	3.1056E-3
23	0.9683	3.1255E-3	−0.0452E-3	3.0803E-3
24	0.9601	3.0991E-3	−0.0440E-3	3.0551E-3
25	0.9519	3.0726E-3	−0.0427E-3	3.0299E-3
26	0.9469	3.0566E-3	−0.0431E-3	3.0135E-3
27	0.9419	3.0403E-3	−0.0435E-3	2.9968E-3
28	0.9369	3.0241E-3	−0.0439E-3	2.9802E-3
29	0.9318	3.0076E-3	−0.0441E-3	2.9635E-3
30	0.9266	2.9911E-3	−0.0443E-3	2.9468E-3
31	0.9250	2.9857E-3	−0.0447E-3	2.9410E-3
32	0.9235	2.9809E-3	−0.0451E-3	2.9358E-3
33	0.9220	2.9762E-3	−0.0455E-3	2.9307E-3
34	0.9205	2.9712E-3	−0.0457E-3	2.9255E-3
35	0.9189	2.9661E-3	−0.0458E-3	2.9203E-3
36	0.9146	2.9521E-3	−0.0464E-3	2.9057E-3
37	0.9102	2.9379E-3	−0.0469E-3	2.8910E-3
38	0.9058	2.9239E-3	−0.0475E-3	2.8764E-3
39	0.9014	2.9095E-3	−0.0478E-3	2.8617E-3
40	0.8969	2.8951E-3	−0.0480E-3	2.8471E-3
41	0.8898	2.8722E-3	−0.0486E-3	2.8236E-3
42	0.8827	2.8491E-3	−0.0491E-3	2.8000E-3
43	0.8755	2.8261E-3	−0.0496E-3	2.7765E-3
44	0.8683	2.8028E-3	−0.0499E-3	2.7529E-3
45	0.8611	2.7795E-3	−0.0501E-3	2.7294E-3
46	0.8593	2.7736E-3	−0.0498E-3	2.7238E-3
47	0.8574	2.7677E-3	−0.0495E-3	2.7182E-3
48	0.8556	2.7618E-3	−0.0492E-3	2.7126E-3
49	0.8538	2.7560E-3	−0.0490E-3	2.7070E-3
50	0.8520	2.7502E-3	−0.0488E-3	2.7014E-3
51	0.8505	2.7454E-3	−0.0485E-3	2.6969E-3
52	0.8491	2.7408E-3	−0.0484E-3	2.6924E-3

Chronological Age, Years	(BMR)std Kcal/Kg hr	$(d_i S/dt)$std Kcal/Kg hr °K	$(d_e S/dt)$std Kcal/Kg hr °K	(dS/dt)std Kcal/Kg hr °K
53	0.8476	2.7361E-3	−0.0482E-3	2.6879E-3
54	0.8462	2.7313E-3	−0.0479E-3	2.6834E-3
55	0.8446	2.7264E-3	−0.0475E-3	2.6789E-3
56	0.8432	2.7217E-3	−0.0473E-3	2.6744E-3
57	0.8418	2.7171E-3	−0.0472E-3	2.6699E-3
58	0.8403	2.7124E-3	−0.0470E-3	2.6654E-3
59	0.8388	2.7076E-3	−0.0467E-3	2.6609E-3
60	0.8373	2.7028E-3	−0.0464E-3	2.6564E-3
61	0.8367	2.7007E-3	−0.0461E-3	2.6546E-3
62	0.8361	2.6988E-3	−0.0460E-3	2.6528E-3
63	0.8354	2.6967E-3	−0.0458E-3	2.6509E-3
64	0.8348	2.6946E-3	−0.0455E-3	2.6491E-3
65	0.8341	2.6925E-3	−0.0452E-3	2.6473E-3
66	0.8331	2.6891E-3	−0.0445E-3	2.6446E-3
67	0.8322	2.6862E-3	−0.0442E-3	2.6420E-3
68	0.8312	2.6831E-3	−0.0438E-3	2.6393E-3
69	0.8302	2.6798E-3	−0.0431E-3	2.6367E-3
70	0.8292	2.6764E-3	−0.0424E-3	2.6340E-3
71	0.8286	2.6745E-3	−0.0417E-3	2.6328E-3
72	0.8281	2.6730E-3	−0.0414E-3	2.6316E-3
73	0.8276	2.6714E-3	−0.0410E-3	2.6304E-3
74	0.8270	2.6695E-3	−0.0403E-3	2.6292E-3
75	0.8264	2.6675E-3	−0.0395E-3	2.6280E-3
76	0.8360	2.6663E-3	−0.0391E-3	2.6272E-3

Source: Guyton, A.C., *Textbook of Medical Physiology,* 4th ed. (Philadelphia: Saunders, 1971).

The expected lifespan, t_f [defined by $d/dt(dS/dt)_{t_f} = 0$], for the five data sources given above are compiled in table 6–13. The expected lifespan, t_f^* [defined by $d/dt\ (d_i S/dt)_{t_f^*} = 0$], is presented in table 6–14. Also in tables 6–13 and 6–14 are the values for entropy production rates in the vicinity of death, $(dS/dt)_{t_f}$ and $(d_i S/dt)_{t_f^*}$. In addition, we present in these two tables the polynomial regression equations for dS/dt and $d_i S/dt$. In appendix A, sample calculations for human males, based on Aub and Du Bois's basal metabolic rate date, are presented.

We calculated composite values for the standard total rate of change of entropy, (dS/dt)std, by averaging the five (dS/dt) curves reported in tables 6–5 through 6–12. The area under the (dS/dt)std curve [that is $\int_0^t (dS/dt)$std dt] can be calculated by trapezoidal integration rules [82],

$$\int_{x_0}^{x_1} f(t)\, dt = \frac{h}{2}\left[f(x_0) + f(x_1) \right] - \frac{h^3}{12} f(\xi) \qquad (6.23)$$

Table 6–7

Standard Values of Basal Metabolic Rate, (BMR)std, Internal Entropy Production Rate, $(d_i S/dt)$std, External Entropy Flow Rate, $(d_e S/dt)$std, and Total Rate of Change of Entropy, (dS/dt)std, for Human Females, Based on Robertson and Reid's Basal Metabolic Rate Data

Chronological Age Years	(BMR)std Kcal/Kg hr	$(d_i S/dt)$std Kcal/Kg hr °K	$(d_e S/dt)$std Kcal/Kg hr °K	(dS/dt)std Kcal/Kg hr °K
6	1.7487	5.6446E-3	−0.1417E-3	5.5029E-3
7	1.6506	5.3280E-3	−0.1240E-3	5.2040E-3
8	1.5206	4.9084E-3	−0.1062E-3	4.8022E-3
9	1.3925	4.4949E-3	−0.0885E-3	4.4064E-3
10	1.2645	4.0817E-3	−0.0707E-3	4.0110E-3
11	1.2100	3.9057E-3	−0.0681E-3	3.8376E-3
12	1.1556	3.7300E-3	−0.0654E-3	3.6646E-3
13	1.1011	3.5543E-3	−0.0628E-3	3.4915E-3
14	1.0467	3.3786E-3	−0.0601E-3	3.3185E-3
15	1.0183	3.2871E-3	−0.0571E-3	3.2300E-3
16	0.9913	3.1997E-3	−0.0541E-3	3.1456E-3
17	0.9642	3.1123E-3	−0.0511E-3	3.0612E-3
18	0.9371	3.0249E-3	−0.0481E-3	2.9768E-3
19	0.9339	3.0144E-3	−0.0472E-3	2.9672E-3
20	0.9309	3.0047E-3	−0.0463E-3	2.9584E-3
21	0.9286	2.9974E-3	−0.0454E-3	2.9520E-3
22	0.9263	2.9900E-3	−0.0445E-3	2.9455E-3
23	0.9238	2.9818E-3	−0.0427E-3	2.9391E-3
24	0.9215	2.9744E-3	−0.0418E-3	2.9326E-3
25	0.9191	2.9671E-3	−0.0409E-3	2.9262E-3
26	0.9182	2.9637E-3	−0.0412E-3	2.9225E-3
27	0.9171	2.9603E-3	−0.0415E-3	2.9188E-3
28	0.9160	2.9568E-3	−0.0418E-3	2.9150E-3
29	0.9149	2.9532E-3	−0.0419E-3	2.9113E-3
30	0.9138	2.9496E-3	−0.0420E-3	2.9076E-3
31	0.9080	2.9310E-3	−0.0423E-3	2.8887E-3
32	0.9022	2.9122E-3	−0.0425E-3	2.8697E-3
33	0.8964	2.8934E-3	−0.0426E-3	2.8508E-3
34	0.8906	2.8747E-3	−0.0429E-3	2.8318E-3
35	0.8848	2.8560E-3	−0.0431E-3	2.8129E-3
36	0.8818	2.8463E-3	−0.0444E-3	2.8019E-3
37	0.8786	2.8359E-3	−0.0450E-3	2.7909E-3
38	0.8753	2.8255E-3	−0.0456E-3	2.7799E-3
39	0.8723	2.8158E-3	−0.0469E-3	2.7689E-3
40	0.8693	2.8060E-3	−0.0481E-3	2.7579E-3
41	0.8673	2.7994E-3	−0.0494E-3	2.7500E-3
42	0.8650	2.7921E-3	−0.0500E-3	2.7421E-3
43	0.8628	2.7849E-3	−0.0506E-3	2.7343E-3
44	0.8607	2.7783E-3	−0.0519E-3	2.7264E-3
45	0.8586	2.7716E-3	−0.0531E-3	2.7185E-3
46	0.8559	2.7626E-3	−0.0518E-3	2.7108E-3
47	0.8533	2.7542E-3	−0.0511E-3	2.7031E-3
48	0.8507	2.7458E-3	−0.0504E-3	2.6954E-3
49	0.8478	2.7367E-3	−0.0490E-3	2.6877E-3
50	0.8450	2.7276E-3	−0.0476E-3	2.6800E-3
51	0.8418	2.7172E-3	−0.0462E-3	2.6710E-3

Chronological Age Years	(BMR)std Kcal/Kg hr	($d_i S/dt$)std Kcal/Kg hr °K	($d_e S/dt$)std Kcal/Kg hr °K	(dS/dt)std Kcal/Kg hr °K
52	0.8390	2.7083E-3	−0.0455E-3	2.6628E-3
53	0.8363	2.6995E-3	−0.0448E-3	2.6547E-3
54	0.8333	2.6899E-3	−0.0434E-3	2.6465E-3
55	0.8304	2.6803E-3	−0.0420E-3	2.6383E-3
56	0.8279	2.6723E-3	−0.0420E-3	2.6303E-3
57	0.8254	2.6644E-3	−0.0420E-3	2.6224E-3
58	0.8230	2.6564E-3	−0.0420E-3	2.6144E-3
59	0.8205	2.6485E-3	−0.0420E-3	2.6065E-3
60	0.8181	2.6406E-3	−0.0421E-3	2.5985E-3
61	0.8157	2.6331E-3	−0.0421E-3	2.5910E-3
62	0.8134	2.6257E-3	−0.0421E-3	2.5836E-3
63	0.8111	2.6182E-3	−0.0421E-3	2.5761E-3
64	0.8088	2.6108E-3	−0.0421E-3	2.5687E-3
65	0.8064	2.6030E-3	−0.0418E-3	2.5612E-3
66	0.8044	2.5966E-3	−0.0416E-3	2.5550E-3
67	0.8024	2.5901E-3	−0.0414E-3	2.5487E-3
68	0.8004	2.5836E-3	−0.0411E-3	2.5425E-3
69	0.7983	2.5768E-3	−0.0406E-3	2.5362E-3
70	0.7962	2.5700E-3	−0.0400E-3	2.5300E-3
71	0.7947	2.5651E-3	−0.0395E-3	2.5256E-3
72	0.7932	2.5602E-3	−0.0389E-3	2.5213E-3
73	0.7916	2.5553E-3	−0.0384E-3	2.5169E-3
74	0.7902	2.5507E-3	−0.0381E-3	2.5126E-3
75	0.7888	2.5460E-3	−0.0378E-3	2.5082E-3

Source: Guyton, A.C., *Textbook of Medical Physiology*, 4th ed. (Philadelphia: Saunders, 1971).

Table 6-8
Standard Values of Basal Metabolic Rate, (BMR)std, Internal Entropy Production Rate, ($d_i S/dt$)std, External Entropy Flow Rate, ($d_e S/dt$)std, and Total Rate of Change of Entropy, (dS/dt)std, for Human Males, Based on Boothby's Basal Metabolic Rate Data

Chronological Age, Years	(BMR)std Kcal/Kg hr	($d_i S/dt$)std Kcal/Kg hr °K	($d_e S/dt$)std Kcal/Kg hr °K	(dS/dt)std Kcal/Kg hr °K
6	1.7456	5.6345E-3	−0.1316E-3	5.5029E-3
7	1.6488	5.3220E-3	−0.1160E-3	5.2060E-3
8	1.5524	5.0111E-3	−0.1004E-3	4.9107E-3
9	1.4562	4.7003E-3	−0.0848E-3	4.6155E-3
10	1.3598	4.3893E-3	−0.0691E-3	4.3202E-3
11	1.3313	4.2973E-3	−0.0681E-3	4.2292E-3
12	1.3028	4.2052E-3	−0.0670E-3	4.1382E-3
13	1.2742	4.1131E-3	−0.0659E-3	4.0472E-3
14	1.2457	4.0210E-3	−0.0648E-3	3.9562E-3
15	1.2148	3.9211E-3	−0.0618E-3	3.8593E-3
16	1.1838	3.8212E-3	−0.0588E-3	3.7624E-3
17	1.1529	3.7213E-3	−0.0558E-3	3.6655E-3

Table 6-8 continued

Chronological Age, Years	(BMR)std Kcal/Kg hr	$(d_iS/dt)std$ Kcal/Kg hr °K	$(d_eS/dt)std$ Kcal/Kg hr °K	$(dS/dt)std$ Kcal/Kg hr °K
18	1.1219	3.6213E-3	− 0.0527E-3	3.5686E-3
19	1.0987	3.5465E-3	− 0.0515E-3	3.4950E-3
20	1.0760	3.4733E-3	− 0.0502E-3	3.4231E-3
21	1.0677	3.4465E-3	− 0.0490E-3	3.3975E-3
22	1.0594	3.4197E-3	− 0.0477E-3	3.3720E-3
23	1.0507	3.3916E-3	− 0.0452E-3	3.3464E-3
24	1.0425	3.3649E-3	− 0.0440E-3	3.3209E-3
25	1.0341	3.3380E-3	− 0.0427E-3	3.2953E-3
26	1.0295	3.3232E-4	− 0.0431E-3	3.2801E-3
27	1.0249	3.3084E-3	− 0.0435E-3	3.2649E-3
28	1.0203	3.2935E-3	− 0.0439E-3	3.2496E-3
29	1.0157	3.2785E-3	− 0.0441E-3	3.2344E-3
30	1.0110	3.2635E-3	− 0.0443E-3	3.2192E-3
31	1.0065	3.2489E-3	− 0.0447E-3	3.2042E-3
32	1.0020	3.2343E-3	− 0.0451E-3	3.1892E-3
33	0.9974	3.2196E-3	− 0.0455E-3	3.1741E-3
34	0.9929	3.2048E-3	− 0.0457E-3	3.1591E-3
35	0.9882	3.1899E-3	− 0.0458E-3	3.1441E-3
36	0.9842	3.1768E-3	− 0.0464E-3	3.1304E-3
37	0.9801	3.1636E-3	− 0.0469E-3	3.1167E-3
38	0.9761	3.1506E-3	− 0.0475E-3	3.1031E-3
39	0.9719	3.1372E-3	− 0.0478E-3	3.0894E-3
40	0.9677	3.1237E-3	− 0.0480E-3	3.0643E-3
41	0.9644	3.1129E-3	− 0.0486E-3	3.0643E-3
42	0.9610	3.1021E-3	− 0.0491E-3	3.0530E-3
43	0.9577	3.0912E-3	− 0.0496E-3	3.0416E-3
44	0.9542	3.0802E-3	− 0.0499E-3	3.0303E-3
45	0.9508	3.0690E-3	− 0.0501E-3	3.0189E-3
46	0.9472	3.0573E-3	− 0.0498E-3	3.0075E-3
47	0.9435	3.0456E-3	− 0.0495E-3	2.9961E-3
48	0.9399	3.0339E-3	− 0.0492E-3	2.9847E-3
49	0.9363	3.0223E-3	− 0.0490E-3	2.9733E-3
50	0.9327	3.0107E-3	− 0.0488E-3	2.9619E-3
51	0.9300	3.0020E-3	− 0.0485E-3	2.9535E-3
52	0.9274	2.9935E-3	− 0.0484E-3	2.9451E-3
53	0.9248	2.9850E-3	− 0.0482E-3	2.9368E-3
54	0.9221	2.9763E-3	− 0.0479E-3	2.9284E-3
55	0.9193	2.9675E-3	− 0.0475E-3	2.9200E-3
56	0.9167	2.9589E-3	− 0.0473E-3	2.9116E-3
57	0.9140	2.9504E-3	− 0.0472E-3	2.9032E-3
58	0.9114	2.9418E-3	− 0.0470E-3	2.8948E-3
59	0.9087	2.9331E-3	− 0.0467E-3	2.8864E-3
60	0.9060	2.9244E-3	− 0.0464E-3	2.8780E-3
61	0.9047	2.9201E-3	− 0.0461E-3	2.8740E-3
62	0.9034	2.9160E-3	− 0.0460E-3	2.8700E-3
63	0.9021	2.9118E-3	− 0.0458E-3	2.8660E-3
64	0.9007	2.9075E-3	− 0.0455E-3	2.8620E-3
65	0.8994	2.9032E-3	− 0.0452E-3	2.8580E-3
66	0.8980	2.8986E-3	− 0.0445E-3	2.8541E-3
67	0.8967	2.8944E-3	− 0.0442E-3	2.8502E-3
68	0.8953	2.8900E-3	− 0.0438E-3	2.8462E-3
69	0.8939	2.8854E-3	− 0.0431E-3	2.8423E-3
70	0.8925	2.8808E-3	− 0.0424E-3	2.8384E-3

Chronological Age Years	(BMR)std Kcal/Kg hr	$(d_iS/dt)std$ Kcal/Kg hr °K	$(d_eS/dt)std$ Kcal/Kg hr °K	$(dS/dt)std$ Kcal/Kg hr °K
71	0.8909	2.8756E-3	−0.0417E-3	2.8339E-3
72	0.8894	2.8708E-3	−0.0414E-3	2.8294E-3
73	0.8879	2.8660E-3	−0.0410E-3	2.8250E-3
74	0.8863	2.8608E-3	−0.0403E-3	2.8205E-3
75	0.8846	2.8555E-3	−0.0395E-3	2.8160E-3
76	0.8832	2.8507E-3	−0.0391E-3	2.8116E-3
77	0.8818	2.8462E-3	−0.0389E-3	2.8073E-3
78	0.8803	2.8415E-3	−0.0386E-3	2.8029E-3
79	0.8788	2.8367E-3	−0.0381E-3	2.7986E-3
80	0.8773	2.8318E-3	−0.0376E-3	2.7942E-3

Source: Guyton, A.C., *Textbook of Medical Physiology,* 4th ed. (Philadelphia: Saunders, 1971).

Table 6–9
Standard Values of Basal Metabolic Rate, (BMR)std, Internal Entropy Production Rate, (d_iS/dt)std, External Entropy Flow Rate, (d_eS/dt)std, and Total Rate of Change of Entropy, (dS/dt)std, for Human Males, Based on Aub and Du Bois's Basal Metabolic Rate Data

Chronological Age Years	(BMR)std Kcal/Kg hr	$(d_iS/dt)std$ Kcal/Kg hr °K	$(d_eS/dt)std$ Kcal/Kg hr °K	$(dS/dt)std$ Kcal/Kg hr °K
16	1.2219	3.9440E-3	−0.0588E-3	3.8852E-3
17	1.1728	3.7858E-3	−0.0558E-3	3.7300E-3
18	1.1245	3.6297E-3	−0.0527E-3	3.5770E-3
19	1.0925	3.5265E-3	−0.0515E-3	3.4750E-3
20	1.0607	3.4237E-3	−0.0502E-3	3.3735E-3
21	1.0549	3.4050E-3	−0.0490E-3	3.3560E-3
22	1.0491	3.3863E-3	−0.0477E-3	3.3386E-3
23	1.0429	3.3663E-3	−0.0452E-3	3.3211E-3
24	1.0371	3.3477E-3	−0.0440E-3	3.3037E-3
25	1.0313	3.3289E-3	−0.0427E-3	3.2862E-3
26	1.0262	3.3124E-3	−0.0431E-3	3.2693E-3
27	1.0211	3.2959E-3	−0.0435E-3	3.2524E-3
28	1.0159	3.2793E-3	−0.0439E-3	3.2354E-3
29	1.0108	3.2626E-3	−0.0441E-3	3.2185E-3
30	1.0056	3.2459E-3	−0.0443E-3	3.2016E-3
31	1.0029	3.2372E-3	−0.0447E-3	3.1925E-3
32	1.0022	3.2349E-3	−0.0451E-3	3.1894E-3
33	1.0003	3.2289E-3	−0.0455E-3	3.1834E-3
34	0.9985	3.2230E-3	−0.0457E-3	3.1773E-3
35	0.9966	3.2170E-3	−0.0458E-3	3.1712E-3
36	0.9951	3.2119E-3	−0.0464E-3	3.1655E-3
37	0.9934	3.2067E-3	−0.0469E-3	3.1598E-3
38	0.9919	3.2016E-3	−0.0475E-3	3.1541E-3
39	0.9902	3.1962E-3	−0.0478E-3	3.1484E-3
40	0.9885	3.1907E-3	−0.0480E-3	3.1427E-3
41	0.9871	3.1862E-3	−0.0486E-3	3.1376E-3
42	0.9857	3.1816E-3	−0.0491E-3	3.1325E-3

Table 6-9 continued

Chronological Age Years	(BMR)std Kcal/Kg hr	$(d_iS/dt)std$ Kcal/Kg hr °K	$(d_eS/dt)std$ Kcal/Kg hr °K	(dS/dt)std Kcal/Kg hr °K
43	0.9842	3.1770E-3	-0.0496E-3	3.1274E-3
44	0.9828	3.1722E-3	-0.0499E-3	3.1223E-3
45	0.9812	3.1673E-3	-0.0501E-3	3.1172E-3
46	0.9797	3.1623E-3	-0.0498E-3	3.1125E-3
47	0.9782	3.1574E-3	-0.0495E-3	3.1079E-3
48	0.9766	3.1524E-3	-0.0492E-3	3.1032E-3
49	0.9751	3.1476E-3	-0.0490E-3	3.0986E-3
50	0.9736	3.1427E-3	-0.0488E-3	3.0939E-3
51	0.9703	3.1320E-3	-0.0485E-3	3.0835E-3
52	0.9670	3.1215E-3	-0.0484E-3	3.0731E-3
53	0.9638	3.1110E-3	-0.0482E-3	3.0628E-3
54	0.9605	3.1003E-3	-0.0479E-3	3.0524E-3
55	0.9571	3.0895E-3	-0.0475E-3	3.0420E-3
56	0.9541	3.0797E-3	-0.0473E-3	3.0324E-3
57	0.9508	3.0692E-3	-0.0472E-3	3.0220E-3
58	0.9476	3.0586E-3	-0.0470E-3	3.0116E-3
59	0.9447	3.0495E-3	-0.0467E-3	3.0028E-3
60	0.9419	3.0404E-3	-0.0464E-3	2.9940E-3
61	0.9389	3.0307E-3	-0.0461E-3	2.9846E-3
62	0.9360	3.0213E-3	-0.0460E-3	2.9753E-3
63	0.9330	3.0117E-3	-0.0458E-3	2.9659E-3
64	0.9301	3.0021E-3	-0.0455E-3	2.9566E-3
65	0.9271	2.9924E-3	-0.0452E-3	2.9472E-3
66	0.9241	2.9828E-3	-0.0445E-3	2.9383E-3
67	0.9213	2.9737E-3	-0.0442E-3	2.9295E-3
68	0.9184	2.9644E-3	-0.0438E-3	2.9206E-3
69	0.9154	2.9549E-3	-0.0431E-3	2.9118E-3
70	0.9125	2.9453E-3	-0.0424E-3	2.9029E-3
71	0.9117	2.9427E-3	-0.0417E-3	2.9010E-3
72	0.9111	2.9409E-3	-0.0414E-3	2.8995E-3
73	0.9105	2.9391E-3	-0.0410E-3	2.8981E-3
74	0.9099	2.9371E-3	-0.0403E-3	2.8968E-3
75	0.9094	2.9355E-3	-0.0395E-3	2.8960E-3

Source: Guyton, A.C., *Textbook of Medical Physiology,* 4th ed. (Philadelphia: Saunders, 1971).

Table 6-10
Standard Values of Basal Metabolic Rate, (BMR)std, Internal Entropy Production Rate, $(d_iS/dt)std$, External Entropy Flow Rate, (d_eS/dt)std, and Total Rate of Change of Entropy, (dS/dt)std, for Human Females, Based on Aub and Du Bois's Basal Metabolic Rate Data

Chronological Age Years	(BMR)std Kcal/Kg hr	$(d_iS/dt)std$ Kcal/Kg hr °K	$(d_eS/dt)std$ Kcal/Kg hr °K	(dS/dt)std Kcal/Kg hr °K
16	1.1684	3.7715E-3	-0.0541E-3	3.7174E-3
17	1.1210	3.6185E-3	-0.0511E-3	3.5647E-3
18	1.0741	3.4670E-3	-0.0481E-3	3.4189E-3
19	1.0455	3.3747E-3	-0.0472E-3	3.3275E-3
20	1.0176	3.2846E-3	-0.0463E-3	3.2383E-3
21	1.0141	3.2734E-3	-0.0454E-3	3.2280E-3
22	1.0107	3.2623E-3	-0.0445E-3	3.2178E-3

Chronological Age, Years	$(BMR)std$ Kcal/Kg hr	$(d_i S/dt)std$ Kcal/Kg hr °K	$(d_e S/dt)std$ Kcal/Kg hr °K	$(dS/dt)std$ Kcal/Kg hr °K
23	1.0069	3.2502E-3	− 0.0427E-3	3.2075E-3
24	1.0035	3.2391E-3	− 0.0418E-3	3.1973E-3
25	1.0000	3.2279E-3	− 0.0409E-3	3.1870E-3
26	0.9970	3.2181E-3	− 0.0412E-3	3.1769E-3
27	0.9940	3.2084E-3	− 0.0415E-3	3.1669E-3
28	0.9909	3.1986E-3	− 0.0418E-3	3.1568E-3
29	0.9879	3.1887E-3	− 0.0419E-3	3.1468E-3
30	0.9848	3.1787E-3	− 0.0420E-3	3.1367E-3
31	0.9818	3.1690E-3	− 0.0423E-3	3.1267E-3
32	0.9787	3.1592E-3	− 0.0425E-3	3.1167E-3
33	0.9787	3.1592E-3	− 0.0425E-3	3.1167E-3
34	0.9727	3.1397E-3	− 0.0429E-3	3.0968E-3
35	0.9696	3.1299E-3	− 0.0431E-3	3.0868E-3
36	0.9670	3.1213E-3	− 0.0444E-3	3.0769E-3
37	0.9641	3.1121E-3	− 0.0450E-3	3.0671E-3
38	0.9613	3.1028E-3	− 0.0456E-3	3.0272E-3
39	0.9586	3.0943E-3	− 0.0469E-3	3.0474E-3
40	0.9559	3.0856E-3	− 0.0481E-3	3.0375E-3
41	0.9531	3.0764E-3	− 0.0494E-3	3.0270E-3
42	0.9501	3.0668E-3	− 0.0500E-3	3.0168E-3
43	0.9472	3.0575E-3	− 0.0506E-3	3.0069E-3
44	0.9445	3.0487E-3	− 0.0519E-3	2.9968E-3
45	0.9419	3.0403E-3	− 0.0531E-3	2.9872E-3
46	0.9385	3.0293E-3	− 0.0518E-3	2.9775E-3
47	0.9352	3.0188E-3	− 0.0511E-3	2.9677E-3
48	0.9320	3.0084E-3	− 0.0504E-3	2.9580E-3
49	0.9285	2.9972E-3	− 0.0490E-3	2.9482E-3
50	0.9251	2.9861E-3	− 0.0476E-3	2.9385E-3
51	0.9214	2.9742E-3	− 0.0462E-3	2.9280E-3
52	0.9181	2.9634E-3	− 0.0455E-3	2.9179E-3
53	0.9148	2.9528E-3	− 0.0448E-3	2.9080E-3
54	0.9113	2.9415E-3	− 0.0434E-3	2.8981E-3
55	0.9078	2.9302E-3	− 0.0420E-3	2.8882E-3
56	0.9047	2.9204E-3	− 0.0420E-3	2.8784E-3
57	0.9017	2.9105E-3	− 0.0420E-3	2.8685E-3
58	0.8986	2.9007E-3	− 0.0420E-3	2.8587E-3
59	0.8956	2.8908E-3	− 0.0420E-3	2.8488E-3
60	0.8926	2.8811E-3	− 0.0421E-3	2.8390E-3
61	0.8911	2.8765E-3	− 0.0421E-3	2.8344E-3
62	0.8897	2.8719E-3	− 0.0421E-3	2.8298E-3
63	0.8883	2.8674E-3	− 0.0421E-3	2.8253E-3
64	0.8869	2.8628E-3	− 0.0421E-3	2.8207E-3
65	0.8854	2.8580E-3	0.0418E-3	2.8162E-3
66	0.8840	2.8534E-3	− 0.0416E-3	2.8118E-3
67	0.8826	2.8488E-3	− 0.0414E-3	2.8074E-3
68	0.8811	2.8441E-3	− 0.0411E-3	2.8030E-3
69	0.8796	2.8392E-3	− 0.0406E-3	2.7986E-3
70	0.8780	2.8342E-3	− 0.0400E-3	2.7942E-3
71	0.8766	2.8295E-3	− 0.0395E-3	2.7900E-3
72	0.8751	2.8247E-3	− 0.0389E-3	2.7858E-3
73	0.8736	2.8198E-3	− 0.0384E-3	2.7814E-3
74	0.8722	2.8153E-3	− 0.0381E-3	2.7772E-3
75	0.8711	2.8118E-3	− 0.0378E-3	2.7740E-3

Source: Guyton A.C., *Textbook of Medical Physiology,* 4th ed. (Philadelphia: Saunders, 1971).

Table 6–11
Standard Values of Basal Metabolic Rate, (BMR)std, Internal Entropy Production Rate, $(d_i S/dt)$std, External Entropy Flow Rate, $(d_e S/dt)$std, and Total Rate of Change of Entropy, (dS/dt)std, for Human Males Based on Fleish's Basal Metabolic Rate Data

Chronological Age Years	(BMR)std Kcal/Kg hr	$(d_i S/dt)$std Kcal/Kg hr °K	$(d_e S/dt)$std Kcal/Kg hr °K	(dS/dt)std Kcal/Kg hr °K
1	2.0830	6.7237E-3	−0.1664E-3	6.5573E-3
2	1.8900	6.1007E-3	−0.1577E-3	6.9430E-3
3	1.7268	5.5738E-3	−0.1534E-3	5.4204E-3
4	1.6047	5.1799E-3	−0.1490E-3	5.0309E-3
5	1.4814	4.7817E-3	−0.1403E-3	4.6414E-3
6	1.3580	4.3835E-3	−0.1316E-3	4.2519E-3
7	1.3261	4.2806E-3	−0.1160E-3	4.1646E-3
8	1.2942	4.1776E-3	−0.1004E-3	4.0772E-3
9	1.2623	4.0747E-3	−0.0848E-3	3.9899E-3
10	1.2304	3.9716E-3	−0.0691E-3	3.9025E-3
11	1.2053	3.8907E-3	−0.0681E-3	3.8226E-3
12	1.1802	3.8096E-3	−0.0670E-3	3.7426E-3
13	1.1551	3.7286E-3	−0.0659E-3	3.6627E-3
14	1.1300	3.6475E-3	−0.0648E-3	3.5827E-3
15	1.1090	3.5798E-3	−0.0618E-3	3.5180E-3
16	1.0880	3.5120E-3	−0.0588E-3	3.4532E-3
17	1.0670	3.4443E-3	−0.0558E-3	3.3885E-3
18	1.0460	3.3764E-3	−0.0527E-3	3.3237E-3
19	1.0379	3.3501E-3	−0.0515E-3	3.2986E-3
20	1.0297	3.3236E-3	−0.0502E-3	3.2734E-3
21	1.0215	3.2973E-3	−0.0490E-3	3.2483E-3
22	1.0133	3.2709E-3	−0.0477E-3	3.2232E-3
23	1.0048	3.2433E-3	−0.0452E-3	3.1981E-3
24	0.9966	3.2169E-3	−0.0440E-3	3.1729E-3
25	0.9884	3.1905E-3	−0.0427E-3	3.1478E-3
26	0.9831	3.1733E-3	−0.0431E-3	3.1302E-3
27	0.9778	3.1561E-3	−0.0435E-3	3.1126E-3
28	0.9725	3.1390E-3	−0.0439E-3	3.0951E-3
29	0.9671	3.1216E-3	−0.0441E-3	3.0775E-3
30	0.9617	3.1042E-3	−0.0443E-3	3.0599E-3
31	0.9564	3.0870E-3	−0.0447E-3	3.0423E-3
32	0.9510	3.0698E-3	−0.0451E-3	3.0247E-3
33	0.9457	3.0527E-3	−0.0455E-3	3.0072E-3
34	0.9403	3.0353E-3	−0.0457E-3	2.9896E-3
35	0.9349	3.0178E-3	−0.0458E-3	2.9720E-3
36	0.9312	3.0059E-3	−0.0464E-3	2.9595E-3
37	0.9275	2.9938E-3	−0.0469E-3	2.9469E-3
38	0.9238	2.9819E-3	−0.0475E-3	2.9344E-3
39	0.9200	2.9696E-3	−0.0478E-3	2.9218E-3
40	0.9162	2.9573E-3	−0.0480E-3	2.9093E-3
41	0.9125	2.9454E-3	−0.0486E-3	2.8968E-3
42	0.9087	2.9333E-3	−0.0491E-3	2.8842E-3
43	0.9050	2.9213E-3	−0.0496E-3	2.8717E-3
44	0.9012	2.9090E-3	−0.0499E-3	2.8591E-3
45	0.8974	2.8967E-3	−0.0501E-3	2.8466E-3

Chronological Age Years	$(BMR)std$ Kcal/Kg hr	$(d_i S/dt)std$ Kcal/Kg hr °K	$(d_e S/dt)std$ Kcal/Kg hr °K	$(dS/dt)std$ Kcal/Kg hr °K
46	0.8942	2.8864E-3	−0.0498E-3	2.8366E-3
47	0.8910	2.8761E-3	−0.0495E-3	2.8266E-3
48	0.8878	2.8657E-3	−0.0492E-3	2.8165E-3
49	0.8846	2.8555E-3	−0.0490E-3	2.8065E-3
50	0.8815	2.8453E-3	−0.0488E-3	2.7965E-3
51	0.8783	2.8350E-3	−0.0485E-3	2.7865E-3
52	0.8751	2.8248E-e	−0.0484E-3	2.7764E-3
53	0.8720	2.8146E-3	−0.0482E-3	2.7664E-3
54	0.8687	2.8042E-3	−0.0479E-3	2.7563E-4
55	0.8655	2.7938E-3	−0.0475E-3	2.7463E-3
56	0.8631	2.7860E-3	−0.0473E-3	2.7387E-3
57	0.8608	2.7784E-3	−0.0472E-3	2.7312E-3
58	0.8583	2.7706E-3	−0.0470E-3	2.7236E-3
59	0.8559	2.7628E-3	−0.0467E-3	2.7161E-3
60	0.8535	2.7549E-3	−0.0464E-3	2.7085E-3
61	0.8510	2.7470E-3	−0.0461E-3	2.7009E-3
62	0.8487	2.7394E-3	−0.0460E-3	2.6934E-3
63	0.8463	2.7316E-3	−0.0458E-3	2.6858E-3
64	0.8438	2.7238E-3	−0.0455E-3	2.6783E-3
65	0.8414	2.7159E-3	−0.0452E-3	2.6707E-3
66	0.8403	2.7124E-3	−0.0445E-3	2.6679E-3
67	0.9393	2.7093E-3	−0.0442E-3	2.6651E-3
68	0.8384	2.7062E-3	−0.0438E-3	2.6624E-3
69	0.8373	2.7027E-3	−0.0431E-3	2.6596E-3
70	0.8362	2.6992E-3	−0.0424E-3	2.6568E-3
71	0.8351	2.6957E-3	−0.0417E-3	2.6540E-3
72	0.8342	2.6926E-3	−0.0414E-3	2.6512E-3
73	0.8332	2.6894E-3	−0.0410E-3	2.6484E-3
74	0.8321	2.6859E-3	−0.0403E-3	2.6456E-3
75	0.8310	2.6823E-3	−0.0395E-3	2.6428E-3
76	0.8304	2.6804E-3	−0.0391E-3	2.6413E-3
77	0.8298	2.6786E-3	−0.0389E-3	2.6397E-3
78	0.8293	2.6768E-3	−0.0386E-3	2.6382E-3
79	0.8268	2.6747E-3	−0.0381E-3	2.6366E-3
80	0.8280	2.6727E-3	−0.0376E-3	2.6351E-3
81	0.8274	2.6707E-3	−0.0371E-3	2.6336E-3
82	0.8268	2.6689E-3	−0.0369E-3	2.6320E-3
83	0.8263	2.6671E-3	−0.0366E-3	2.6305E-3
84	0.8256	2.6650E-3	−0.0361E-1	2.6289E-3
85	0.8251	2.6633E-3	−0.0359E-3	2.6274E-3
86	0.8246	2.6618E-3	−0.0357E-3	2.6261E-e
87	0.8241	2.6602E-3	−0.0355E-3	2.6247E-3
88	0.8238	2.6590E-3	−0.0351E-3	2.6239E-3
89	0.8231	2.6569E-3	−0.0349E-3	2.6220E-3
90	0.8226	2.6554E-3	−0.0347E-3	2.6207E-3

Source: Guyton, A.C., *Textbook of Medical Physiology,* 4th ed. (Philadelphia: Saunders, 1971).

Table 6-12
Standard Values of Basal Metabolic Rate, (BMR)std, Internal Entropy Production Rate, (d_iS/dt)std, External Entropy Flow Rate, (d_eS/dt)std, and Total Rate of Change of Entropy, (dS/dt)std, for Human Females, Based on Fleish's Basal Metabolic Rate Data

Chronological Age, Years	(BMR)std Kcal/Kg hr	(d_iS/dt)std Kcal/Kg hr °K	(d_eS/dt)std Kcal/Kg hr °K	(dS/dt)std Kcal/Kg hr °K
1	2.0830	6.7237E-3	−0.1783E-3	6.5454E-3
2	1.8597	6.0030E-3	−0.1692E-3	5.8338E-3
3	1.6840	5.4356E-3	−0.1646E-3	5.2710E-3
4	1.5479	4.9965E-3	−0.1600E-3	4.8365E-3
5	1.4112	4.5551E-3	−0.1509E-3	4.4042E-3
6	1.2820	4.1382E-3	−0.1417E-3	3.9965E-3
7	1.2548	4.0503E-3	−0.1240E-3	3.9263E-3
8	1.2275	3.9623E-3	−0.1062E-3	3.8561E-3
9	1.2003	3.8743E-3	−0.0885E-3	3.7858E-3
10	1.1730	3.7863E-3	−0.0707E-3	3.7156E-3
11	1.1504	3.7135E-3	−0.0681E-3	3.6454E-3
12	1.1279	3.6406E-3	−0.0654E-3	3.5752E-3
13	1.1053	3.5677E-3	−0.0628E-3	3.5049E-3
14	1.0827	3.4948E-3	−0.0601E-3	3.4347E-3
15	1.0600	3.4216E-3	−0.0571E-3	3.3645E-3
16	1.0373	3.3484E-3	−0.0541E-3	3.2943E-3
17	1.0146	3.2751E-3	−0.0511E-3	3.2240E-3
18	0.9920	3.2019E-3	−0.0481E-3	3.1538E-3
19	0.9861	3.1812E-3	−0.0472E-3	3.1340E-3
20	0.9791	3.1604E-3	−0.0463E-3	3.1141E-3
21	0.9727	3.1397E-3	−0.0454E-3	3.0943E-3
22	0.9663	3.1190E-3	−0.0445E-3	3.0745E-3
23	0.9596	3.0974E-3	−0.0427E-3	3.0547E-3
24	0.9531	3.0766E-3	−0.0418E-3	3.0348E-3
25	0.9467	3.0559E-3	−0.0409E-3	3.0150E-3
26	0.9442	3.0476E-3	−0.0412E-3	3.0064E-3
27	0.9416	3.0393E-3	−0.0415E-3	2.9978E-3
28	0.9390	3.0309E-3	−0.0418E-3	2.9891E-3
29	0.9363	3.0224E-3	−0.0419E-3	2.9805E-3
30	0.9337	3.0139E-3	−0.0420E-3	2.9719E-3
31	0.9311	3.0056E-3	−0.0423E-3	2.9633E-3
32	0.9285	2.9972E-3	−0.0425E-3	2.9547E-3
33	0.9259	2.9886E-3	−0.0426E-3	2.9460E-3
34	0.9233	2.9803E-3	−0.0429E-3	2.9374E-3
35	0.9207	2.9719E-3	−0.0431E-3	.9288E-3
36	0.9180	2.9633E-3	−0.0444E-3	2.9189E-3
37	0.9152	2.9540E-3	−0.0450E-3	2.9090E-3
38	0.9122	2.9446E-3	−0.0456E-3	2.8990E-3
39	0.9096	2.9360E-3	−0.0469E-3	2.8891E-3
40	0.9069	2.9273E-3	−0.0481E-3	2.8792E-3
41	0.9042	2.9187E-3	−0.0494E-3	2.8693E-3
42	0.9013	2.9094E-3	−0.0500E-3	2.8594E-3
43	0.8984	2.9000E-3	−0.0506E-3	2.8494E-3
44	0.8958	2.8914E-3	−0.0519E-3	2.8395E-3
45	0.8930	2.8826E-3	−0.0531E-3	2.8295E-3
46	0.8897	2.8719E-3	−0.0518E-3	2.8201E-3

Chronological Age, Years	(BMR)std Kcal/Kg hr	$(d_i S/dt)std$ Kcal/Kg hr °K	$(d_e S/dt)std$ Kcal/Kg hr °K	$(dS/dt)std$ Kcal/Kg hr °K
47	0.8866	2.8619E-3	− 0.0511E-3	2.8108E-3
48	0.8835	2.8518E-3	− 0.0504E-3	2.8014E-3
49	0.8802	2.8411E-3	− 0.0490E-3	2.7921E-3
50	0.8768	2.8303E-3	− 0.0476E-3	2.7827E-3
51	0.8735	2.8195E-3	− 0.0462E-3	2.7733E-3
52	0.8704	2.8095E-3	− 0.0455E-3	2.7640E-3
53	0.8673	2.7994E-3	− 0.0448E-3	2.7546E-3
54	0.8639	2.7887E-3	− 0.0434E-3	2.7453E-3
55	0.8606	2.7779E-3	− 0.0420E-3	2.7359E-3
56	0.8581	2.7697E-3	− 0.0420E-3	2.7277E-3
57	0.8555	2.7615E-3	− 0.0420E-3	2.7195E-3
58	0.8530	2.7533E-3	− 0.0420E-3	2.7113E-3
59	0.8504	2.7451E-3	− 0.0420E-3	2.7031E-3
60	0.8479	2.7370E-3	− 0.0421E-3	2.6949E-3
61	0.8454	2.7288E-3	− 0.0421E-3	2.6867E-3
62	0.8428	2.7206E-3	− 0.0421E-3	2.6785E-3
63	0.8403	2.7123E-3	− 0.0421E-3	2.6702E-3
64	0.8390	2.7083E-3	− 0.0421E-3	2.6620E-3
65	0.8351	2.6956E-3	− 0.0418E-3	2.6538E-3
66	0.8338	2.6913E-3	− 0.0416E-3	2.6497E-3
67	0.8324	2.6870E-3	− 0.0414E-3	2.6456E-3
68	0.8310	2.6825E-3	− 0.0411E-3	2.6414E-3
69	0.8296	2.6779E-3	− 0.0406E-3	2.6373E-3
70	0.8282	2.6732E-3	− 0.0400E-3	2.6332E-3
71	0.8267	2.6686E-3	− 0.0395E-3	2.6291E-3
72	0.8253	2.6639E-3	− 0.0389E-3	2.6250E-3
73	0.8238	2.6592E-3	− 0.0384E-3	2.6208E-3
74	0.8225	2.6548E-3	− 0.0381E-3	2.6167E-3
75	0.8211	2.6504E-3	− 0.0378E-3	2.6126E-3
76	0.8203	2.6478E-3	− 0.0372E-3	2.6106E-3
77	0.8195	2.6452E-3	− 0.0366E-3	2.6086E-3
78	0.8187	2.6425E-3	− 0.0360E-3	2.6065E-3
79	0.8184	2.6402E-3	− 0.0357E-3	2.6045E-3
80	0.8172	2.6378E-3	− 0.0353E-3	2.6025E-3
81	0.8164	2.6352E-3	− 0.0347E-3	2.6005E-3
82	0.8155	2.6324E-3	− 0.0340E-3	2.5984E-3
83	0.8147	2.6298E-3	− 0.0334E-3	2.5964E-3
84	0.8140	2.6274E-3	− 0.0331E-3	2.5943E-3
85	0.8132	2.6250E-3	− 0.0327E-3	2.5923E-3
86	0.8125	2.6227E-3	− 0.0324E-3	2.5903E-3
87	0.8118	2.6204E-3	− 0.0321E-3	2.5883E-3
88	0.8111	2.6181E-3	− 0.0319E-3	2.5862E-3
89	0.8104	2.6158E-3	− 0.0316E-3	2.5842E-3
90	0.8097	2.6135E-3	− 0.0313E-3	2.5822E-3

Source: Guyton, A.C., *Textbook of Medical Physiology,* 4th ed. (Philadelphia: Saunders, 1971).

Table 6–13
Expected Lifespan, t_f, Total Entropy Production Rate in the Vicinity of Death $(dS/dt)t_f$, and Polynomial Regression Equations dS/dt, for Human Males and Females, Based on Basal Metabolic Rate Data of Various Sources

BMR Data Sources	t_f Years	$(dS/dt)\,t_f$ Kcal/Kg hr °K	Polynomial Regression Equation of dS/dt Kcal/Kg hr °K
Shock's male data	75.1	2.6094E-3	$(3.876E{-}3) - (3.374E{-}5)t + (2.247E{-}7)t^2,\ t > 20$
Robertson's male data	77.0	2.6268E-3	$(3.597E{-}3) - (2.522E{-}5)t + (1.639E{-}7)t^2,\ t > 20$
Robertson's female data	102.3	2.4316E-3	$(3.274E{-}3) - (1.646E{-}5)t + (0.804E{-}7)t^2,\ t > 20$
Boothby's male data	84.7	2.7797E-3	$(3.854E{-}3) - (2.538E{-}5)t + (1.499E{-}7)t^2,\ t > 20$
Aub and Du Bois's male data	76.2	2.8957E-3	$(4.119E{-}3) - (3.212E{-}5)t + (2.108E{-}7)t^2,\ t > 16$
Aub and Du Bois's female data	76.3	2.773E-3	$(3.960E{-}3) - (3.111E{-}5)t + (2.038E{-}7)t^2,\ t > 16$
Fleish's male data	107.8	2.6081E-3	$6.557E{-}3$ $0 < t < 1$ $(6.703E{-}3) - (3.886E{-}4)t + (1.072E{-}5)t^2,\ 1 < t < 20$ $(3.532E{-}3) - (1.718E{-}5)t + (0.797E{-}7)t^2,\ t > 20$
Fleish's female data	109.9	2.5615E-3	$6.545E{-}3$ $0 < t < 1$ $(6.683E{-}3) - (4.216E{-}4)t + (1.193E{-}5)t^2,\ 1 < t < 20$ $(3.370E{-}3) - (1.472E{-}5)t + (0.670E{-}7)t^2,\ t > 20$

Sources: N. W. Shock et al., "Age Differences in the Water Content of the Body Related to Basal Oxygen Consumption in Males," *J. Gerontol.* 18 (1963):1; Guyton, A.C., *Textbook of Medical Physiology*, 4th ed. (Philadelphia: Saunders, 1971).

Table 6-14
Expected Lifespan, t_f, Internal Entropy Production Rate in the Vicinity of Death, $(d_iS/dt)_{t_f}^*$, and Polynomial Regression Equations, for d_iS/dt, for Human Males and Females, Based on Basal Metabolic Rate Data of Various Sources

BMR Data Sources	t_f^* Years	$(d_iS/dt)_{t_f}^*$ KcalKg hr °K	Polynomial Regression Equation of dS/dt Kcal/Kg hr °K
Shock's male data	76.8	2.6483E-3	$(3.895E\text{-}3) - (3.251E\text{-}5)t + (2.118E\text{-}7)t^2, t > 20$
Robertson's male data	77.5	2.6655E-3	$(3.638E\text{-}3) - (2.495E\text{-}5)t + (1.610E\text{-}7)t^2, t > 20$
Robertson's female data	106.7	2.4321E-3	$(3.304E\text{-}3) - (1.562E\text{-}5)t + (0.705E\text{-}7)t^2, t > 20$
Boothby's male data	86.8	2.8153E-3	$(3.899E\text{-}3) - (2.531E\text{-}5)t + (1.457E\text{-}7)t^2, t > 20$
Aub and Du Bois's male data	76.7	2.9345E-3	$(4.176E\text{-}3) - (3.232E\text{-}5)t + (2.107E\text{-}7)t^2, t > 16$
Aub and Du Bois's female data	77.1	2.8094E-3	$(4.010E\text{-}3) - (3.108E\text{-}5)t + (2.015E\text{-}7)t^2, t > 16$
Fleish's male data	108.5	2.6390E-3	$6.272E\text{-}3, \quad 0 < t < 1$ $(6.885E\text{-}3) - (1.621E\text{-}5)t + (1.101E\text{-}5)t^2, 1 < t < 20$ $(3.557E\text{-}3) - (1.621E\text{-}5)t + (0.696E\text{-}7)t^2, \quad t > 20$
Fleish's female data	111.0	2.5865E-3	$6.724E\text{-}3, \quad 0 < t < 1$ $(6.881E\text{-}3) - (4.361E\text{-}4)t + (1.227E\text{-}5)t^2, 1 < t < 20$ $(3.394E\text{-}3) - (1.377E\text{-}7)t + (0.568E\text{-}7)t^2, \quad t > 20$

Sources: N.W. Shock et al., "Age Differences in the Water Content of the Body Related to Basal Oxygen Consumption in Males," *J. Gerontol.* 18 (1963):1; Guyton, A.C., *Textbook of Medical Physiology*, 4th ed. (Philadelphia: Saunders, 1971).

The results of these calculations for (BMR)std, (d_iS/dt)std, (d_eS/dt)std, (dS/dt)std, $(dS/dt)t_f$, $(d_iS/dt)\overset{*}{i_f}$, $\int_0^t(d_iS/dt)$std dt, and $\int_0^t(dS/dt)$std dt are shown in tables 6–15 and 6–16 for human males and females. Sample calculations are shown in appendixes A through D.

The expected lifespan, t_f, for the composite data is 84.2 years for males and 96.2 years for females. The expected lifespan, $t\overset{*}{f}$, for the composite data is 85 years for males and 98 years for females. The definition of t_f relates to the hypothesis that a living organism in the course of its life evolves toward a stationary state (senile death) which may correspond to a minimum critical level of entropy production, that is, $d/dt(dS/dt)t_f = 0$. The lifetime accumulation of total entropy based on the composite curves $[\int_0^{t_f}(dS/dt)$std $dt = K]$ is 2,395 Kcal/Kg°K for males and 2,551 Kcal/Kg°K for females. The lifetime accumulation of internal entropy based on the composite curves $[\int_0^{t_f}(d_iS/dt)$std $dt = K^*]$ is 2,456 Kcal/Kg°K for males and 2,635 Kcal/Kg°K for females. The composite plot of (BMR)std versus t is shown in figure 6–5 for human males and females. The plot of expected lifespan versus age based on the published data of Metropolitan Life Insurance Company [68] is shown in figure 6–6, where the ultimate lifespan is found to be 103 years for males and 109 years for females. The composite plots of (d_iS/dt)std and (dS/dt)std versus chronological age are shown in figures 6–7 and 6–8 for human males and females.

It is interesting to compare Calloway's estimate [13] of the critical BMR value for humans (the lowest value which can support life) with that projected from Metropolitan Life data and our composite BMR versus age figures. Calloway gives a critical BMR value of 0.833 Kcal/Kg hr for human males. At the ultimate lifespan for Metropolitan Life data of 103 years, this translates from table 6–15 into a critical BMR value for males of 0.840 Kcal/Kg hr. For our composite curves, the critical BMR value for males is approximately 0.845 Kcal/Kg hr, at the ultimate lifespan, $t\overset{*}{f}$, of 85 years.

We also tabulated the critical level of entropy production in the vicinity of death, $(dS/dt)_{t_f}$, and support the idea that it too may be a fixed value. From table 6–15, we see this is apparently true where we show an average value for males of 2.691E-3 Kcal/Kg hr °K. Parallel calculations were done for $t\overset{*}{f}$ and $(d_iS/dt)\overset{*}{i_f}$. These results yield similar conclusions and are shown in table 6–15.

Entropic Age and Expected Lifespan

As mentioned before, we designed and constructed a whole–body calorimeter which can measure basal metabolic rates, (BMR)exp, for human subjects. With these data and equation 6.14, we can obtain the internal entropy generation rate, (d_iS/dt)exp. From table 6–15 (or table 6–16; for

Table 6-15
The Composite Standard Values of Basal Metabolic Rate (BMR), Internal Entropy Production Rate (d_iS/dt), External Entropy Flow Rate (d_eS/dt), Total Rate of Change of Entropy (dS/dt), Accumulation of Internal Entropy Production [$\int_0^t (d_iS/dt)dt$], and Accumulation of Total Entropy Generation [$\int_0^t (dS/dt)dt$], for Human Males

CA, Years	$(BMR)std$[a] Kcal/Kg hr	$(d_iS/dt)std$ Kcal/Kg hr °K	$(d_eS/dt)std$[b] Kcal/Kg hr °K	$(dS/dt)std$ Kcal/Kg hr °K	$\int_0^t (d_iS/dt)std\,dt$ Kcal/Kg °K	$\int_0^t (dS/dt)std\,dt$ Kcal/Kg °K
1	2.0830	6.7237E-3	-0.1664E-3	6.5573E-3	29.4498	28.7170
2	1.9686	6.3582E-3	-0.1577E-3	6.2005E-3	86.7485	84.5962
3	1.8576	5.9962E-3	-0.1534E-3	5.8428E-3	140.8608	137.3472
4	1.7456	5.6345E-3	-0.1490E-3	5.4855E-3	191.8033	186.9647
5	1.6875	5.4472E-3	-0.1403E-3	5.3069E-3	240.3412	233.9402
6	1.6295	5.2598E-3	-0.1316E-3	5.1282E-3	287.2379	279.8820
7	1.5495	5.0017E-3	-0.1160E-3	4.8857E-3	332.1833	323.3824
8	1.4688	4.7411E-3	-0.1004E-3	4.6407E-3	374.8568	365.1080
9	1.3896	4.4854E-3	-0.0848E-3	4.4006E-3	415.2689	404.7094
10	1.3096	4.2272E-3	-0.0691E-3	4.1581E-3	453.4301	442.1969
11	1.2831	4.1418E-3	-0.0681E-3	4.0737E-3	490.0863	478.2522
12	1.2378	3.9955E-3	-0.0670E-3	3.9285E-3	525.7277	513.3018
13	1.2019	3.8796E-3	-0.0659E-3	3.8137E-3	560.2206	547.2127
14	1.1660	3.7636E-3	-0.0648E-3	3.6988E-3	593.6978	580.1179
15	1.1539	3.7246E-3	-0.0618E-3	3.6628E-3	626.4961	612.3617
16	1.1418	3.6856E-3	-0.0588E-3	3.6268E-3	658.9528	644.2901
17	1.1106	3.5848E-3	-0.0558E-3	3.5290E-3	690.7972	675.6325
18	1.0793	3.4838E-3	-0.0527E-3	3.4311E-3	721.7577	706.1182
19	1.0741	3.4671E-3	-0.0515E-3	3.4156E-3	752.2026	736.1068
20	1.0689	3.4502E-3	-0.0502E-3	3.4000E-3	782.5004	765.9591
21	1.0560	3.4086E-3	-0.0490E-3	3.3596E-3	812.5419	795.5661
22	1.0429	3.3663E-3	-0.0477E-3	3.3186E-3	842.2160	824.8166
23	1.0294	3.3228E-3	-0.0452E-3	3.2776E-3	871.5143	853.7080
24	1.0160	3.2796E-3	-0.0440E-3	3.2356E-3	900.4328	882.2358
25	1.0042	3.2415E-3	-0.0427E-3	3.1988E-3	928.9952	910.4185
26	0.9968	3.2175E-3	-0.0431E-3	3.1744E-3	957.2856	938.3331
27	0.9893	3.1933E-3	-0.0435E-3	3.1498E-3	985.3649	966.0331
28	0.9819	3.1694E-3	-0.0439E-3	3.1255E-3	1013.2335	993.5189

Table 6–15 continued

CA, Years	$(BMR)_{std}$ Kcal/Kg hr	$(d_iS/dt)_{std}$ Kcal/Kg hr °K	$(d_eS/dt)_{std}$ Kcal/Kg hr °K	$(dS/dt)_{std}$ Kcal/Kg hr °K	$\int_0^t (d_iS/dt)_{std}\,dt$ Kcal/Kg °K	$\int_0^t (dS/dt)_{std}\,dt$ Kcal/Kg °K
29	0.9781	3.1573E-3	−0.0441E-3	3.1132E-3	1040.9445	1020.8444
30	0.9744	3.1451E-3	−0.0443E-3	3.1008E-3	1068.5490	1048.0617
31	0.9692	3.1283E-3	−0.0447E-3	3.0836E-3	1096.0265	1075.1494
32	0.9647	3.1140E-3	−0.0451E-3	3.0689E-3	1123.3678	1102.0974
33	0.9604	3.1000E-3	−0.0455E-3	3.0545E-3	1150.5851	1128.9179
34	0.9570	3.0891E-3	−0.0457E-3	3.0457E-3	1177.6934	1155.6267
35	0.9536	3.0780E-3	−0.0458E-3	3.0322E-3	1204.7053	1182.2378
36	0.9494	3.0645E-3	−0.0464E-3	3.0181E-3	1231.6095	1208.7381
37	0.9455	3.0518E-3	−0.0469E-3	3.0049E-3	1258.3989	1235.1188
38	0.9415	3.0391E-3	−0.0475E-3	2.9916E-3	1285.0770	1261.3835
39	0.9392	3.0316E-3	−0.0478E-3	2.9838E-3	1311.6667	1287.5558
40	0.9368	3.0239E-3	−0.0480E-3	2.9759E-3	1338.1898	1313.6593
41	0.9316	3.0071E-3	−0.0486E-3	2.9585E-3	1364.6056	1339.6520
42	0.9266	2.9909E-3	−0.0491E-3	2.9585E-3	1390.8768	1365.4953
43	0.9216	2.9748E-3	−0.0496E-3	2.9252E-3	1417.0066	1391.1928
44	0.9187	2.9655E-3	−0.0499E-3	2.9156E-3	1443.0251	1416.7755
45	0.9158	2.9562E-3	−0.0501E-3	2.9061E-3	1468.9622	1442.2746
46	0.9130	2.9472E-3	−0.0498E-3	2.8974E-3	1494.8191	1467.6939
47	0.9106	2.9393E-3	−0.0495E-3	2.8898E-3	1520.6020	1493.0418
48	0.9090	2.9317E-3	−0.0492E-3	2.8825E-3	1546.3170	1518.3245
49	0.9062	2.9251E-3	−0.0490E-3	2.8761E-3	1571.9698	1543.5472
50	0.9242	2.9186E-3	−0.0488E-3	2.8698E-3	1597.5652	1568.7142
51	0.9007	2.9072E-3	−0.0485E-3	2.8587E-3	1623.0822	1593.8050
52	0.8986	2.9006E-3	−0.0484E-3	2.8522E-3	1648.5204	1618.8187
53	0.8960	2.8923E-3	−0.0482E-3	2.8441E-3	1673.8933	1643.7685
54	0.8938	2.8852E-3	−0.0479E-3	2.8373E-3	1699.1988	1668.6530
55	0.8916	2.8779E-3	−0.0475E-3	2.8304E-3	1724.4412	1693.4775
56	0.8889	2.8691E-3	−0.0473E-3	2.8218E-3	1749.6131	1718.2341
57	0.8863	2.8609E-3	−0.0472E-3	2.8137E-3	1774.7105	1742.9176
58	0.8837	2.8525E-3	−0.0470E-3	2.8055E-3	1799.7352	1767.5297
59	0.8817	2.8461E-3	−0.0467E-3	2.7994E-3	1824.6951	1792.0792

60	0.8797	2.8396E-3	−0.0464E-3	2.7932E-3	1849.5985	1816.5748
61	0.8726	2.8167E-3	−0.0461E-3	2.7706E-3	1874.3731	1840.9442
62	0.8700	2.8084E-3	−0.0460E-3	2.7624E-3	1899.0110	1865.1787
63	0.8674	2.8000E-3	−0.0458E-3	2.7542E-3	1923.5758	1889.3414
64	0.8657	2.7944E-3	−0.0455E-3	2.7489E-3	1948.0793	1913.4450
65	0.8640	2.7888E-3	−0.0452E-3	2.7436E-3	1972.5337	1937.5022
66	0.8633	2.7865E-3	−0.0445E-3	2.7420E-3	1996.9535	1961.5291
67	0.8626	2.7845E-3	−0.0442E-3	2.7403E-3	2021.3545	1985.5416
68	0.8620	2.7824E-3	−0.0438E-3	2.7386E-3	2045.7375	2009.5392
69	0.8615	2.7809E-3	−0.0431E-3	2.7378E-3	2070.1048	2033.5258
70	0.8610	2.7793E-3	−0.0424E-3	2.7369E-3	2094.4585	2057.5050
71	0.8603	2.7770E-3	−0.0417E-3	2.7353E-3	2118.7951	2081.4732
72	0.8597	2.7750E-3	−0.0414E-3	2.7336E-3	2143.1129	2105.4270
73	0.8590	2.7729E-3	−0.0410E-3	2.7319E-3	2167.4127	2129.3659
74	0.8586	2.7714E-3	−0.0403E-3	2.7311E-3	2191.6967	2153.2938
75	0.8581	2.7697E-3	−0.0395E-3	2.7302E-3	2215.9667	2177.2143
76	0.8555	2.7614E-3	−0.0391E-3	2.7223E-3	2240.1929	2201.0963
77	0.8533	2.7544E-3	−0.0389E-3	2.7155E-3	2264.3521	2224.9139
78	0.8511	2.7474E-3	−0.0386E-3	2.7088E-3	2288.4500	2248.6723
79	0.8494	2.7416E-3	−0.0381E-3	2.7035E-3	2312.4918	2272.3782
80	0.8476	2.7358E-3	−0.0376E-3	2.6982E-3	2336.4828	2296.0377
81	0.8467	2.7330E-3	−0.0371E-3	2.6959E-3	2360.4361	2319.6639
82	0.8459	2.7304E-3	−0.0369E-3	2.6935E-3	2384.3658	2343.2819
83	0.8451	2.7278E-3	−0.0366E-3	2.6912E-3	2408.2727	2366.7669
84	0.8449	2.7271E-3	−0.0361E-3	2.6910E-3	2432.1652	2390.3409
84.2[c]	0.8449	2.7271E-3	−0.0361E-3	2.6910E-3	2436.9429	2395.0555
85[d]	0.8448	2.7269E-3	−0.0359E-3	2.6910E-3	2456.0537	2413.9140

Source: H. Faseb. "Respiration and Circulation," Federation of American Societies for Experimental Biology (Bethesda, 1971).

[a] Composite of Shock, Robertson, Boothby, Du Bois, and Fleish's data.

[b] Based on an average weight per person's age according to Faseb's data.

[c] t_f age where $(d/dt)(dS/dt) = 0$ from figure 6–7.

[d] t_f^* age where $(d/dt)(d_i S/dt) = 0$ from figure 6–7.

Table 6-16
The Composite Standard Values of Basal Metabolic Rate, (BMR), Internal Entropy Production Rate, (d_iS/dt), External Entropy Flow Rate, (d_eS/dt), Total Rate of Change of Entropy, (dS/dt), Accumulation of Internal Entropy Production, $[\int_0^t (d_iS/dt)dt]$, and Accumulation of Total Entropy Generation, $[\int_0^t (dS/dt)dt]$, for Human Females

CA, Years	(BMR)std[a] Kcal/Kg hr	(d_iS/dt)std Kcal/Kg hr °K	(d_eS/dt)std[b] Kcal/Kg hr °K	(dS/dt)std Kcal/Kg hr °K	$\int_0^t (d_iS/dt)$ std dt Kcal/Kg °K	$\int_0^t (dS/dt)$std dt Kcal/Kg °K
1	2.0830	6.7237E-3	−0.1783E-3	6.5454E-3	29.4498	28.6689
2	1.8828	6.0774E-3	−0.1692E-3	5.9082E-3	85.5186	83.2156
3	1.7827	5.7542E-3	−0.1646E-3	5.5896E-3	137.3410	133.5760
4	1.6825	5.4310E-3	−0.1600E-3	5.2710E-3	186.3322	181.1454
5	1.4823	4.7847E-3	−0.1509E-3	4.6338E-3	231.0770	224.5284
6	1.4631	4.7227E-3	−0.1417E-3	4.5810E-3	272.7194	264.8893
7	1.4413	4.6522E-3	−0.1240E-3	4.5282E-3	313.7815	304.7876
8	1.3671	4.4128E-3	−0.1062E-3	4.3066E-3	353.4862	343.4840
9	1.2930	4.1735E-3	−0.0885E-3	4.0850E-3	391.0942	380.2392
10	1.2188	3.9340E-3	−0.0707E-3	3.8633E-3	426.6051	415.0532
11	1.1576	3.7365E-3	−0.0681E-3	3.6684E-3	460.2019	448.0425
12	1.0964	3.5389E-3	−0.0654E-3	3.4735E-3	492.0682	479.3244
13	1.0816	3.4914E-3	−0.0628E-3	3.4286E-3	522.8609	509.5561
14	1.0723	3.4613E-3	−0.0601E-3	3.4012E-3	553.3137	539.4706
15	1.0671	3.4446E-3	−0.0571E-3	3.3875E-3	583.5615	569.2055
16	1.0534	3.4001E-3	−0.0541E-3	3.3460E-3	613.5413	598.6982
17	1.0396	3.3556E-3	−0.0511E-3	3.3045E-3	643.1313	627.8274
18	1.0258	3.3111E-3	−0.0481E-3	3.2630E-3	673.2092	656.5931
19	1.0126	3.2687E-3	−0.0472E-3	3.2215E-3	702.0287	684.9952
20	0.9995	3.2263E-3	−0.0463E-3	3.1800E-3	730.4768	713.0338
21	0.9901	3.1960E-3	−0.0454E-3	3.1506E-3	758.6065	740.7618
22	0.9808	3.1658E-3	−0.0445E-3	3.1213E-3	786.4712	768.2327
23	0.9711	3.1346E-3	−0.0427E-3	3.0919E-3	814.0670	795.4465
24	0.9617	3.1044E-3	−0.0418E-3	3.0626E-3	841.3938	822.4032
25	0.9524	3.0741E-3	−0.0409E-3	3.0332E-3	868.4556	849.1028
26	0.9465	3.0552E-3	−0.0412E-3	3.0140E-3	895.3019	875.5895
27	0.9407	3.0363E-3	−0.0415E-3	2.9948E-3	921.9827	901.9080
28	0.9348	3.0174E-3	−0.0418E-3	2.9756E-3	948.4979	928.0584
29	0.9289	2.9983E-3	−0.0419E-3	2.9564E-3	974.8467	954.0406
30	0.9230	2.9792E-3	−0.0420E-3	2.9372E-3	1001.0282	979.8546

31	1005.5188	1027.0616	2.9222E-3	−0.0423E-3	2.9645E-3	0.9184
32	1031.0511	1052.9654	2.9071E-3	−0.0425E-3	2.9496E-3	0.9138
33	1056.4516	1078.7386	2.8921E-3	−0.0426E-3	2.9347E-3	0.9092
34	1081.7203	1104.3818	2.8770E-3	−0.0429E-3	2.9199E-3	0.9046
35	1106.8571	1129.8953	2.8620E-3	−0.0431E-3	2.9051E-3	0.9000
36	1131.8910	1155.3124	2.8535E-3	−0.0444E-3	2.8979E-3	0.8978
37	1156.8504	1180.6634	2.8450E-3	−0.0450E-3	2.8900E-3	0.8953
38	1181.7358	1205.9456	2.8366E-3	−0.0456E-3	2.8822E-3	0.8929
39	1206.5472	1231.1621	2.8281E-3	−0.0469E-3	2.8750E-3	0.8907
40	1231.5573	1256.3151	2.8196E-3	−0.0481E-3	2.8677E-3	0.8884
41	1256.2312	1281.4160	2.8137E-3	−0.0494E-3	2.8631E-3	0.8870
42	1280.8534	1306.4735	2.8078E-3	−0.0500E-3	2.8578E-3	0.8854
43	1305.4235	1331.4842	2.8018E-3	−0.0506E-3	2.8524E-3	0.8837
44	1329.9414	1356.4511	2.7959E-3	−0.0519E-3	2.8478E-3	0.8823
45	1354.4076	1381.3772	2.7900E-3	−0.0531E-3	2.8431E-3	0.8808
46	1378.8226	1406.2517	2.7842E-3	−0.0518E-3	2.8360E-3	0.8786
47	1403.1868	1431.0666	2.7784E-3	−0.0511E-3	2.8295E-3	0.8766
48	1427.5002	1455.8246	2.7726E-3	−0.0504E-3	2.8230E-3	0.8746
49	1451.7628	1480.5225	2.7668E-3	−0.0409 −3	2.8158E-3	0.8723
50	1475.9746	1505.1574	2.7610E-3	−0.0476E-3	2.8086E-3	0.8701
51	1500.1347	1529.7283	2.7550E-3	−0.0462E-3	2.8012E-3	0.8678
52	1524.2422	1554.2375	2.7490E-3	−0.0455E-3	2.7945E-3	0.8657
53	1548.2967	1578.6875	2.7429E-3	−0.0448E-3	2.7877E-3	0.8636
54	1572.2982	1603.0753	2.7369E-3	−0.0434E-3	2.7803E-3	0.8613
55	1596.2472	1627.3983	2.7309E-3	−0.0420E-3	2.7729E-3	0.8590
56	1620.1432	1651.6622	2.7248E-3	−0.0420E-3	2.7668E-3	0.8572
57	1643.9857	1675.8727	2.7187E-3	−0.0420E-3	2.7607E-3	0.8553
58	1667.7748	1700.0297	2.7126E-3	−0.0420E-3	2.7546E-3	0.8534
59	1691.5105	1724.1333	2.7065E-3	−0.0420E-3	2.7485E-3	0.8515
60	1715.1927	1748.1839	2.7004E-3	−0.0421E-3	2.7425E-3	0.8496
61	1738.8303	1772.1902	2.6963E-3	−0.0421E-3	2.7384E-3	0.8484
62	1762.4319	1796.1606	2.6922E-3	−0.0421E-3	2.7343E-3	0.8471
63	1785.9881	1820.0956	2.6882E-3	−0.0421E-3	2.7303E-3	0.8459
64	1809.5188	1843.9951	2.6841E-3	−0.0421E-3	2.7262E-3	0.8446
65	1833.0136	1867.8573	2.6800E-3	−0.4118E-3	2.7218E-3	0.8432
66	1856.4729	1891.6819	2.6760E-3	−0.0416E-3	2.7176E-3	0.8419
67	1879.8976	1915.4701	2.6721E-3	−0.0414E-3	2.7135E-3	0.8406
68	1903.2877	1939.2215	2.6681E-3	−0.0411E-3	2.7092E-3	0.8393
69	1926.6432	1962.9348	2.6642E-3	−0.0406E-3	2.7048E-3	0.8380
70	1949.9641	1986.6087	2.6602E-3	−0.0400E-3	2.7002E-3	0.8365

Table 6-16 continued

CA, Years	(BMR)std Kcal/Kg hr	$(d_iS/dt)std$ Kcal/Kg hr °K	$(d_eS/dt)std$ Kcal/Kg hr °K	$(dS/dt)std$ Kcal/Kg hr °K	$\int_0^t (d_iS/dt)std\ dt$ Kcal/Kg °K	$\int_0^t (dS/dt)std\ dt$ Kcal/Kg °K
71	0.8351	2.6957E-3	-0.0395E-3	2.5662E-3	2010.2427	1973.2499
72	0.8337	2.6910E-3	-0.0389E-3	2.6521E-3	2033.8365	1996.5003
73	0.8323	2.6865E-3	-0.0384E-3	2.6481E-3	2057.3900	2019.7152
74	0.8309	2.6821E-3	-0.0183E-3	2.6440E-3	2080.9045	2042.8946
75	0.8296	2.6778E-3	-0.0378E-3	2.6400E-3	2104.3809	2066.0385
76	0.8282	2.6733E-3	-0.0372E-3	2.6361E-3	2127.8187	2089.1478
77	0.8268	2.6688E-3	-0.0366E-3	2.6322E-3	2151.2171	2112.2230
78	0.8254	2.6642E-3	-0.0360E-3	2.6282E-3	2174.5756	2135.2636
79	0.8241	2.6600E-3	-0.0357E-3	2.6243E-3	2197.8956	2158.2696
80	0.8227	2.6557E-3	-0.0353E-3	2.6204E-3	2221.1784	2181.2414
81	0.8222	2.6539E-3	-0.0347E-3	2.6192E-3	2244.4344	2204.1909
82	0.8216	2.6519E-3	-0.0340E-3	2.6179E-3	2267.6738	2227.1294
83	0.8210	2.6501E-3	-0.0334E-3	2.6167E-3	2290.8966	2250.0570
84	0.8205	2.6485E-3	-0.0331E-3	2.6154E-3	2314.1045	2272.9736
85	0.8200	2.6469E-3	-0.0327E-3	2.6142E-3	2337.2984	2295.8793
86	0.8180	2.6404E-3	-0.0274E-3	2.6130E-3	2360.4568	2318.7744
87	0.8160	2.6340E-3	-0.0222E-3	2.6118E-3	2383.5587	2341.6590
88	0.8140	2.6275E-3	-0.0169E-3	2.6106E-3	2406.6041	2364.5331
89	0.8130	2.6243E-3	-0.0149E-3	2.6094E-3	2429.6070	2387.3967
90	0.8120	2.6211E-3	-0.0129E-3	2.6082E-3	2452.5819	2410.2498
91	0.8112	2.6185E-3	-0.0114E-3	2.6071E-3	2475.5314	2433.0928
92	0.8104	2.6159E-3	-0.0099E-3	2.6060E-3	2498.4581	2455.9262
93	0.8096	2.6133E-3	-0.0082E-3	2.6051E-3	2521.3620	2478.7508
94	0.8088	2.6107E-3	-0.0069E-3	2.6044E-3	2544.2431	2501.5684
95	0.8082	2.6088E-3	-0.0049E-3	2.6039E-3	2567.1045	2524.3808
96	0.8078	2.6075E-3	-0.0039E-3	2.6036E-3	2589.9519	2547.1897
96.2[c]	0.8077	2.6072E-3	-0.0037E-3	2.6035E-3	2594.5196	2551.7511
97	0.8076	2.6068E-3	-0.0033E-3	2.6035E-3	2612.7905	2569.9964
98[d]	0.8075	2.6065E-3	-0.0030E-3	2.6035E-3	2635.6248	2592.8031

Source: H. Faseb, "Respiration and Circulation," Federation of American Societies for Experimental Biology (Bethesda, 1971).

[a] Composite of Robertson, Du Bois, and Fleish's data.

[b] Based on an average weight per person's age according to Faseb's data.

[c] t_f age where $(d/dt)(dS/dt) = 0$ from figure 6-7.

[d] t_f^* age where $(d/dt)(d_iS/dt) = 0$ from figure 6-7.

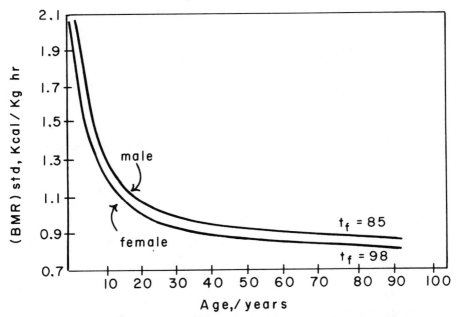

Figure 6-5. Plot of Standard Basal Metabolic Rate versus Age Based on the Composite Data of Shock, Robertson, Boothby, Aub and Du Bois, and Fleish

these calculations, either table can be used), we can find $(d_e S/dt)$std by finding the value as a function of the chronological age. Thus, we can get (dS/dt)exp for human subjects from equation 6.2. The values of $(d_i S/dt)$std and (dS/dt)std can be obtained by interpolation from table 6-15 as a function of the chronological age.

The wear–and–tear (rate of living) theory of aging [4] states that the body has a programmed amount of life "substance" which is used up as a function of life and living. When we deplete the life substance or if the residual amount drops to some critical level, or if the rate at which we consume it diminishes to some sensitive mark, we are sufficiently weakened and die.

Based on these ideas, we believe the lifetime entropy accumulation is a constant. So we have

$$\int_0^{t_{f,exp}} (dS/dt)exp\, dt = \int_0^{t_{f,std}} (dS/dt)std\, dt = K \qquad (6.24)$$

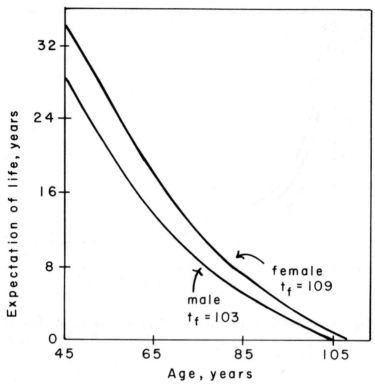

Source: Metropolitan Life Insurance Co., *Statist. Bull.* 50 (July-September 1978): 8-9.
Figure 6-6. Plot of Expectation of Life versus Age Based on the Published
Data of Metropolitan Life Insurance Company

where

(dS/dt)exp = total rate of change of entropy of a human subject at
chronological age, t

$t_{f,\text{exp}}$ = expected lifespan of a human subject

(dS/dt)std = standard total rate of change of entropy of a human
subject at chronological age, t (from pooled data)

$t_{f,\text{std}}$ = standard lifespan for a human subject (where
$d/dt[(dS/dt)\text{std}] = 0$, from pooled data)

K = lifetime accumulation of entropy of humans.
In figure 6-9, a graphical explanation of equation 6.24 is shown.

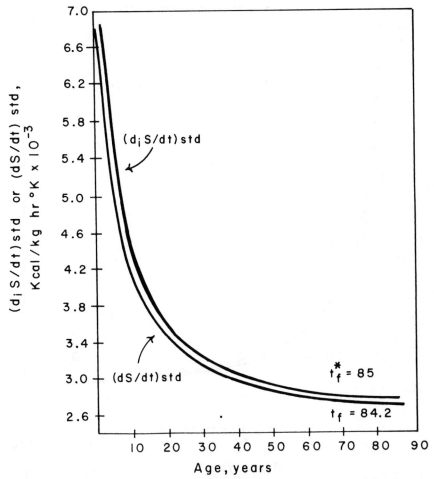

Sources: N.W. Shock et al., "Age Differences in the Water Content of the Body Related to Basal Oxygen Consumption in Males," *J. Gerontol.* 18 (1963):1; and A.C. Guyton, *Textbook of Medical Physiology,* 4th ed. (Saunders, 1971).

Figure 6–7. Plots of (dS/dt) std and $(d_i S/dt)$ std for Human Males Based on the Composite Data of Shock, Robertson, Boothby, Aub and Du Bois, and Fleish

Now, we define an entropic age (EA) as

$$\int_0^{EA} (dS/dt)\text{std } dt = \int_0^{CA} (dS/dt)\exp dt = A \qquad (6.25)$$

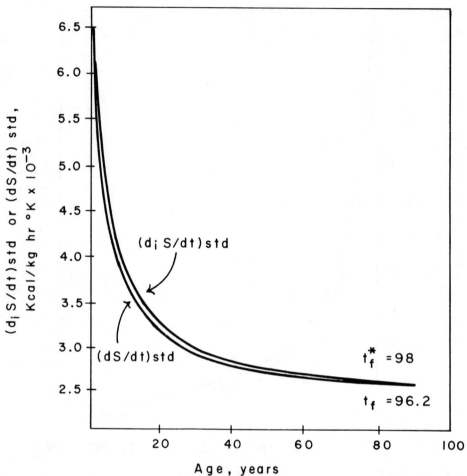

Figure 6-8. Plots of (dS/dt) and (d_iS/dt)std for Human Females Based on the Composite Data of Robertson, Aub and Du Bois, and Fleish

where

    CA = chronological age

    A = total entropy accumulation up to age CA

In figure 6–10, a graphical explanation of equation 6.25 is shown.
It is difficult to know a priori the (dS/dt)exp history for an individual.

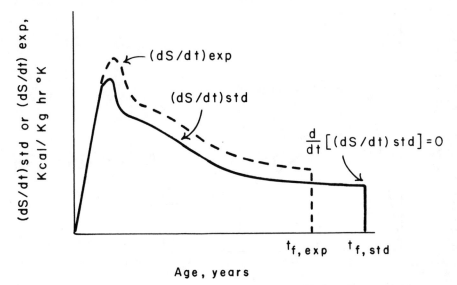

Figure 6-9. A Graphical Explanation of Constant Lifetime Entropy Accumulation, Equation 6.24

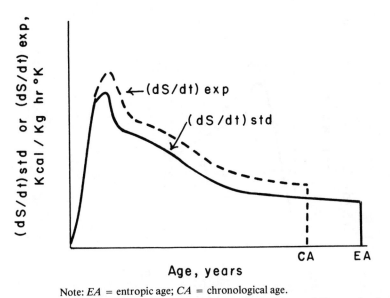

Note: *EA* = entropic age; *CA* = chronological age.

Figure 6-10. A Graphical Explanation of the Definition of Entropic Age, Equation 6.25

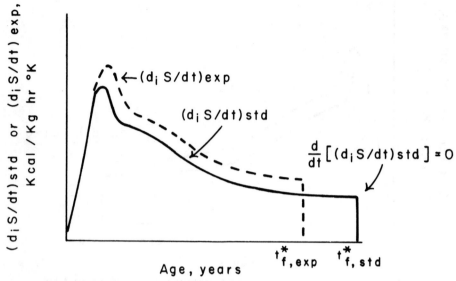

Figure 6–11. A Graphical Explanation of Constant Lifetime Internal Entropy Generation, Equation 6.29

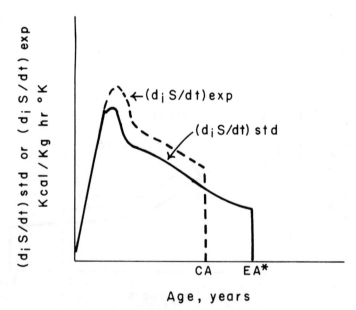

Note: EA^* = entropic age; CA = chronological age.

Figure 6–12. A Graphical Explanation of the Definition of Entropic Age, Equation 6.30

However, if we assume the curve trend of (dS/dt)exp is similar to (dS/dt)std, we may assume

$$(dS/dt)\text{exp} = k1 \times (dS/dt)\text{std} \qquad (6.26)$$

where $k1$ is a proportionality factor.

Let

A = area under the (dS/dt)std curve to age EA

$\quad = \int_0^{EA} (dS/dt)\text{std}\, dt$

$A1$ = area under the (dS/dt)std curve up to age CA

$\quad = \int_0^{CA} (dS/dt)\text{std}\, dt$

then from equations 6.25 and 6.26 we get

$$A = k1 \int_0^{CA} (dS/dt)\text{std}\, dt = k1 \times A1 \qquad (6.27)$$

Thus we can calculate $k1$ from equation 6.26 once (dS/dt)exp and (dS/dt)std are known. $A1$ can be obtained from table 6–15 with CA as parameter. Therefore, we get A from equation 6.27, $A = k1 \times A1$, and go to table 6–15 to find the EA value which makes equation 6.27 true (find t in table 6–15 which corresponds to the A value).

We also define

Af = area under the (dS/dt)std curve up to age $t_{f,\text{exp}}$

$\quad = \int_0^{t_{f,\text{exp}}} (dS/dt)\text{std}\, dt$

Substituting equation 6.26 into equation 6.24, we get

$$Af = \int_0^{t_{f,\text{exp}}} (dS/dt)\text{std}\, dt = K/k1 \qquad (6.28)$$

Once K and $k1$ are known, we go to table 6–15 to find the $t_{f,\text{exp}}$ value which makes equation 6.28 true (find t in table 6–15 which corresponds to the Af value). Then $(dS/dt)_{t_{f,\text{std}}}$ can be obtained from table 6–15 once $t_{f,\text{exp}}$ is known (find the (dS/dt)std value in table 6–15 which corresponds to the CA value that equals $t_{f,\text{exp}}$). We can then calculate the total rate of change of entropy in the vicinity of death for human subjects, $(dS/dt)_{t_{f,\text{exp}}}$, from equation 6.26. One sample calculation is listed in appendix B.

Using the whole-body calorimeter basal metabolic rates, (BMR)exp, for human subjects and equation 6.14, we can obtain the internal entropy generation rate, $(d_i S/dt)$exp,. From table 6–15, we can find $(d_i S/dt)$std by finding the values as a function of the chronological age.

In a parallel procedure we develop analogous equations to equations 6.24 through 6.28, but this time for $d_i S/dt$ and the hypothesis that total lifetime internal entropy generation is a constant. Therefore, we have

$$\int_0^{t^*_{f,\text{exp}}} (d_i S/dt)\text{exp}\, dt = \int_0^{t^*_{f,\text{std}}} (d_i S/dt)\text{std}\, dt = K^* \qquad (6.29)$$

where

$(d_i S/dt)$exp = internal entropy generation rate of a human subject at chronological age, t

$t^*_{f,\text{exp}}$ = expected lifespan of a human subject

$(d_i S/dt)$std = standard internal entropy generation rate of a human subject at chronological age, t (from pooled data)

$t^*_{f,\text{std}}$ = standard lifespan of human subjects
(where $d/dt[(d_i S/dt)$std$] = 0$ from pooled data)

K^* = lifetime accumulation of entropy due to internal generation of humans

In figure 6–11, a graphical explanation of equation 6.29 is shown.

Now we define an entropic age (EA^*) as

$$\int_0^{EA^*} (d_i S/dt)\text{std}\, dt = \int_0^{CA} (d_i S/dt)\text{exp}\, dt = A^* \qquad (6.30)$$

where

CA = chronological age
A^* = internal entropy generation up to age CA

In figure 6–12, a graphical explanation of equation 6.30 is shown.

It is also difficult to know a priori the $(d_i S/dt)$exp history for an individual. However, if we assume the curve trend of $(d_i S/dt)$exp is similar to $(d_i S/dt)$std, we may assume

$$(d_i S/dt)\text{exp} = k1^* \times (d_i S/dt)\text{std} \qquad (6.31)$$

where $k1^*$ is a proportionality factor.

Let

A^* = area under the $(d_i S/dt)$std curve to age EA^*

$$= \int_0^{EA^*} (d_i S/dt) \text{std } dt$$

$A1^* =$ area under the $(d_i S/dt)$std curve up to age CA

$$= \int_0^{CA} (d_i S/dt) \text{std } dt$$

then from equations 6.30 and 6.31 we get

$$A^* = k1^* \int_0^{CA} (d_i S/dt) \text{std } dt = k1^* \times A1^* \qquad (6.32)$$

We can calculate $k1^*$ from equation 6.31 once $(d_i S/dt)$exp and $(d_i S/dt)$std are known. $A1^*$ can be obtained from table 6–15 with CA as the parameter. Therefore we get A^* from equation 6.32 $A^* = k1^* \times A1^*$, and go to table 6–15 to find the EA^* value which makes equation 6.32 true (find t in table 6–15 which corresponds to the A^* value).

We also define

$Af^* =$ area under the $(d_i S/dt)$std curve up to age $t_{f,exp}^*$

$$= \int_0^{t_{f,exp}^*} (d_i S/dt) \text{std } dt$$

Substituting equation 6.31 into equation 6.29, we get

$$Af^* = \int_0^{t_{f,exp}^*} (d_i S/dt) \text{std } dt = K^*/k1^* \qquad (6.33)$$

Thus we can get Af^* from equation 6.33 once K^* and $k1^*$ are known. Then we go to table 6–15 to find the $t_{f,exp}^*$ value which makes equation 6.33 true (find t in table 6–15 which corresponds to the Af^* value). Then $(d_i S/dt)_{f,std}^*$ can be obtained from table 6–15 once $t_{f,exp}^*$ is known (find the $(d_i S/dt)$std value in table 6–15 which corresponds to the CA value that equals $t_{f,exp}^*$). We can then calculate the internal rate of change of entropy in the vicinity of death for human subjects, $(d_i S/dt)_{f,exp}^*$, from equation 6.31. One sample calculation is listed in appendix B.

Summary of Results

We applied the principle of irreversible thermodynamics for open systems to analyze the human body. The irreversibilities of living processes were accounted for by an internal entropy generation rate, measured by the basal metabolic rate, and an external entropy flow rate, calculated from respiration data. The total rate of change of entropy and the internal entropy generation rate for human males were obtained from five different basal metabolic rate data sources (Shock [70], Robertson [31], Boothby [31], Aub and Du Bois [31], and Fleish [31]) and pooled to yield standard values; for human females, we used three different sources of basal metabolic rate data (Robertson [31], Aub and Du Bois [31], and Fleish [31]) and pooled them to yield standard values.

The basal metabolic rate in the vicinity of death for human males and females were obtained for each source of basal metabolic rate data and for the pooled data. These values for males were 0.820, 0.826, 0.872, 0.909, and 0.818, where the pooled value was 0.845 (Kcal/Kg hr) and for females, 0.754, 0.870, and 0.801, where the pooled value was 0.808 (Kcal/Kg hr). Calloway's (BMR) $t^*_{f,std}$ value is 0.833 Kcal/Kg hr. The agreement between our calculations and Calloway's results are interestingly close.

The expected lifespan, $t_{f,exp}$ for human males and females was obtained for each source of basal metabolic rate data and for the pooled data. These values for males were 75.1, 77.0, 84.7, 76.2, and 107.8, where the pooled value was 84.2 (years) and for females, 102.3, 76.3, and 109.9, where the pooled value was 96.2 (years). The expected lifespan, $t^*_{f,exp}$, for human males and females were obtained for each source of basal metabolic rate data and for the pooled data. These values for males were 76.8, 77.5, 86.8, 76.7, and 108.5, where the pooled value was 85 (years) and for females, 106.7, 77.1, and 111, where the pooled value was 98 (years). The expected lifespan based on the published data of the Metropolitan Life Insurance Company is found to be 103 years for human males and 109 years for females.

The lifetime accumulation of total entropy is 2,395 Kcal/Kg °K for human males and 2,551 Kcal/Kg °K for human females. The lifetime accumulation of internal entropy is 2,456 Kcal/Kg °K for human males and 2,635 Kcal/Kg °K for human females.

The total rate of change of entropy in the vicinity of death for human males and females were obtained for each literature source of basal metabolic rate data and for the pooled data. These values for males were 2.609K-3, 2.627E-3, 2.780E-3, 2.896E-3, and 2.608E-3, where the pooled value was 2.691E-3 (Kcal/Kg hr °K) and for females 2.432E-3, 2.773E-3, and 2.562E-3, where the pooled value was 2.604E-3 (Kcal/Kg hr °K). The internal entropy production rate in the vicinity of death for human males and females were obtained for each source of basal metabolic rate data published in the literature and for the pooled data. These values for males were 2.648E-3, 2.666E-3, 2.815E-3, 2.935E-3, and 2.639E-3, where the pooled value was 2.727E-3 (Kcal/Kg hr °K) and for females, 2.432E-3, 2.809E-3, and 2.587E-3, where the pooled value was 2.607E-3 (Kcal/Kg hr °K).

For other values of human subjects found through longitudinal studies at the University of Cincinatti, see tables 6–17 and 6–18.

Table 6–17
The Calculated Basal Metabolic Rate, (BMR)exp, Standard Basal Metabolic Rate, (BMR)std, Entropic Age, EA, Expected Lifespan, $t_{f,exp}$, and Total Rate of Change of Entropy in the Vicinity of Death, $(dS/dt)'_{f,exp}$, for Human Subjects in the University of Cincinnati Longitudinal Study

Subject Index	CA, Years	(BMR)exp Kcal/Kg hr	(BMR)std Kcal/Kg hr	EA, Years	$t_{f,exp}$ Years	$(dS/dt)'_{f,exp}$ Kcal/Kg hr °K
M1–1	25.42	0.8074	1.0011	19.17	109.02	2.163E-3
M2–1	23.75	0.9023	1.0194	19.68	97.58	2.378E-3
M3–1	71.25	0.8408	0.8602	69.27	86.57	2.630E-3
M3–2	71.50	0.8003	0.8600	65.33	91.93	2.501E-3
M3–3	71.75	0.8544	0.8599	71.19	84.85	2.674E-3
M3–4	72.01	0.8424	0.8597	70.22	86.32	2.636E-3
M4–1	44.33	0.9299	0.9177	45.17	82.86	2.728E-3
M4–2	44.83	0.8775	0.9163	4241	88.78	2.575E-3
M4–3	45.17	0.9761	0.9153	49.03	77.79	2.893E-3
M4–4	45.37	0.9044	0.9148	44.71	85.39	2.660E-3
M4–5	46.37	0.9104	0.9121	46.26	84.39	2.686E-3
M5–1	64.58	0.8941	0.8647	67.36	80.80	2.790E-3
M5–2	65.08	0.8742	0.8630	66.06	82.99	2.724E-3
M6–1	22.17	0.9696	1.0406	20.22	91.75	2.505E-3
F1–1	63.96	0.7772	0.8447	57.75	106.08	2.392E-3
F1–2	64.21	0.8760	0.8443	67.16	92.10	2.705E-3
F1–3	64.42	0.8436	0.8440	64.38	96.23	2.602E-3
F1–4	64.83	0.8298	0.8434	63.55	98.08	2.561E-3
F1–5	65.05	0.8879	0.8431	69.28	90.48	2.748E-3
F2–1	64.42	0.8930	0.8436	69.00	89.98	2.762E-3
F2–2	64.83	0.9170	0.8434	70.07	87.25	2.839E-3
F2–3	65.06	0.8331	0.8431	62.67	97.57	2.572E-3
F3–1	23.67	0.9436	0.9648	23.00	98.75	2.545E-3
F4–1	74.81	0.7290	0.8299	63.91	111.94	2.283E-3
F5–1	65.83	0.8819	0.8421	69.63	91.08	2.732E-3
F5–2	66.67	0.9100	0.8120	73.36	87.61	2.829E-3
F5–3	66.90	0.8744	0.8407	70.16	86.62	2.717E-3

Table 6–17 continued

Subject Index	CA, Years	(BMR)exp Kcal/Kg hr	(BMR)std Kcal/Kg hr	EA, Years	$t_{f,exp}$ Years	$(dS/dt)_{f,exp}$ Kcal/Kg hr °K
F5-4	67.10	0.9368	0.8405	76.52	84.56	2.919E-3
F5-5	67.42	0.8360	0.8401	67.02	91.38	2.594E-3
F5-6	67.67	0.8195	0.8397	65.69	99.01	2.540E-3
F5-7	67.94	0.8940	0.8394	73.33	89.28	2.781E-3
F5-8	68.17	0.9199	0.8391	76.20	86.25	2.868E-3
F5-9	68.40	0.9279	0.8388	77.29	85.32	2.896E-3
F6-1	48.33	0.8459	0.8738	46.41	99.96	2.519E-3
F7-1	85.07	0.9172	0.8199	97.14	84.24	2.929E-3
F8-1	32.25	0.8705	0.9127	29.54	101.69	2.482E-3
F8-2	32.58	0.9243	0.9111	32.27	97.06	2.584E-3
F8-3	32.83	0.9417	0.9100	34.31	92.38	2.698E-3
F8-4	33.17	1.0787	0.9084	41.26	78.38	3.126E-3
F8-5	33.33	0.8641	0.9077	31.29	101.93	2.477E-3
F8-6	33.75	0.9517	0.9058	35.96	90.72	2.742E-3
F8-7	33.83	0.8937	0.9054	33.27	97.69	2.569E-3
F9-1	44.92	0.6025	0.8809	27.57	149.36	1.765E-3
F10-1	78.25	0.8097	0.8251	76.50	98.34	2.555E-3
F11-1	65.92	0.7084	0.8420	53.31	117.70	2.184E-3
F11-2	66.08	0.7466	0.8418	57.04	110.73	2.304E-3
F11-3	66.50	0.7463	0.8413	57.42	110.70	2.305E-3
F11-4	66.83	0.7588	0.8408	58.94	108.51	2.346E-3
F11-5	67.02	0.7868	0.8406	61.82	103.98	2.434E-3
F11-6	67.25	0.7065	0.8403	54.33	117.83	2.182E-3
F11-7	67.54	0.7231	0.8399	56.22	114.60	2.236E-3
F11-8	67.83	0.7698	0.8395	61.01	106.51	2.384E-3
F12-1	53.41	0.8269	0.8627	50.69	101.12	2.494E-3
F13-1	71.02	0.8163	0.8351	69.09	98.81	2.544E-3

Source: Wang, H.H., *Entropy Analysis of the Human System*, Ph.D. dissertation, University of Cincinnati, Cincinnati, 1979.

Table 6-18

The Calculated Basal Metabolic Rate, (BMR)exp. Standard Basal Metabolic Rate, (BMR)std, Entropic Age, EA*, Expected Lifespan, $t^*_{f,exp}$, and the Internal Entropy Generation Rate in the Vicinity of Death, $(d_iS/dt)_{t^*_{f,exp}}$, for Human Subjects in the University of Cincinnati Longitudinal Study

Subject Index	CA, Years	(BMR)exp Kcal/Kg hr	(BMR)std Kcal/Kg hr	EA Years	$t^*_{f,exp}$ Years	$(d_iS/dt)_{t^*_{f,exp}}$ Kcal/Kg hr°K
M1-1	25.42	0.8074	1.0011	19.22	109.67	2.199E-3
M2-1	23.75	0.9023	1.0194	20.27	98.35	2.414E-3
M3-1	71.25	0.8408	0.8602	69.29	87.37	2.666E-3
M3-2	71.50	0.8003	0.8600	65.43	92.67	2.538E-3
M3-3	71.75	0.8544	0.8599	71.19	85.66	2.710E-3
M3-4	72.01	0.8424	0.8597	70.24	87.11	2.672E-3
M4-1	44.33	0.9299	0.9177	54.08	83.65	2.764E-3
M4-2	44.83	0.8775	0.9163	42.45	89.54	2.612E-3
M4-3	45.17	0.9761	0.9153	48.97	78.61	2.926E-3
M4-4	45.37	0.9044	0.9148	44.72	86.19	2.696E-3
M4-5	46.37	0.9104	0.9121	46.26	85.20	2.722E-3
M5-1	64.58	0.8941	0.8647	67.31	81.62	2.824E-3
M5-2	65.08	0.8742	0.8639	66.04	83.27	2.760E-3
M6-1	22.17	0.9696	1.0406	20.23	92.53	2.541E-3
F1-1	63.96	0.7772	0.8447	57.82	108.03	2.398E-3
F1-2	64.21	0.8760	0.8443	67.13	93.82	2.709E-3
F1-3	64.42	0.8436	0.8440	64.38	98.06	2.605E-3
F1-4	64.83	0.8298	0.8434	63.57	99.89	2.565E-3
F1-5	65.05	0.8879	0.8431	69.23	92.19	2.754E-3
F2-1	64.42	0.8930	0.8436	68.99	91.62	2.770E-3
F2-2	64.83	0.9170	0.8434	71.69	88.76	2.854E-3
F2-3	65.06	0.8331	0.8431	64.13	99.39	2.576E-3
F3-1	23.67	0.9436	0.9648	23.00	100.60	2.549E-3
F4-1	74.81	0.7290	0.8299	64.02	113.98	2.290E-3
F5-1	65.83	0.8819	0.8421	69.59	92.79	2.738E-3
F5-2	66.67	0.9100	0.8410	73.29	89.26	2.839E-3
F5-3	66.90	0.8744	0.8407	70.14	93.55	2.717E-3

Table 6–18 continued

Subject Index	CA, Years	(BMR)exp Kcal/Kg hr	(BMR)std Kcal/Kg	EA* Years	$t^*_{f,exp}$ Years	$(d_iS/dt)_{t^*_{f,exp}}$ Kcal/Kg hr °K
F5-4	67.10	0.9368	0.8405	76.42	86.18	2.942E-3
F5-5	67.42	0.8360	0.8401	67.02	98.57	2.594E-3
F5-6	67.67	0.8195	0.8397	65.71	100.85	2.544E-3
F5-7	67.94	0.8939	0.8394	73.26	90.99	2.789E-3
F5-8	68.17	0.9199	0.8391	76.11	87.89	2.881E-3
F5-9	68.40	0.9279	0.8388	77.19	86.96	2.914E-3
F6-1	48.33	0.8459	0.8738	46.44	101.80	2.523E-3
F7-1	85.07	0.9172	0.8199	97.17	85.81	2.955E-3
F8-1	32.25	0.8705	0.9127	30.36	103.59	2.486E-3
F8-2	32.58	0.9243	0.9111	33.18	96.35	2.645E-3
F8-3	32.83	0.9417	0.9100	34.29	94.12	2.701E-3
F8-4	33.17	1.0787	0.9084	41.19	79.93	3.154E-3
F8-5	33.33	0.8641	0.9077	31.31	103.82	2.481E-3
F8-6	33.75	0.9517	0.9058	35.93	92.44	2.581E-3
F8-7	33.83	0.8937	0.9054	33.28	99.51	2.573E-3
F9-1	44.92	0.6025	0.8809	27.81	151.34	1.783E-3
F10-1	78.25	0.8097	0.8251	76.51	100.20	2.558E-3
F11-1	65.92	0.7084	0.8420	53.46	119.78	2.193E-3
F11-2	66.08	0.7466	0.8418	57.15	112.72	2.312E-3
F11-3	66.50	0.7463	0.8413	57.53	112.69	2.312E-3
F11-4	66.83	0.7588	0.8408	59.04	110.47	2.352E-3
F11-5	67.02	0.7868	0.8406	61.88	105.89	2.440E-3
F11-6	67.25	0.7065	0.8403	54.51	119.86	2.192E-3
F11-7	67.54	0.7231	0.8399	56.35	116.65	2.244E-3
F11-8	67.83	0.7698	0.8395	61.10	108.45	2.390E-3
F12-1	53.41	0.8269	0.8627	50.72	103.00	2.498E-3
F13-1	71.02	0.8163	0.8351	69.11	100.66	2.548E-3

Source: Wang, H.H., Entropy Analysis of the Human System, Ph.D. dissertation, University of Cincinnati, 1979.

7 A Whole-Body Calorimeter

This chapter discusses the design of a whole-body calorimeter to measure the basal metabolic rate of elderly human subjects.

The whole-body calorimeter, shown in figure 7-1, is a rectangular, transparent, plexiglass box, 7 feet long, 3 feet wide, and 2 feet high. It is a two-piece construction, with a 3/8-inch-thick wall. The lower section is a cushioned slab of plastic resting on supports which extend 3 feet above the floor level. The enclosing section is lowered and raised by an electrical-chain hoist. This enclosing section makes an airtight connection with compressible rubber gasketing. Air flows into and out of the calorimeter, as shown in figure 7-1. Two aspects of the whole-body calorimeter are shown in figures 7-2 and 7-3.

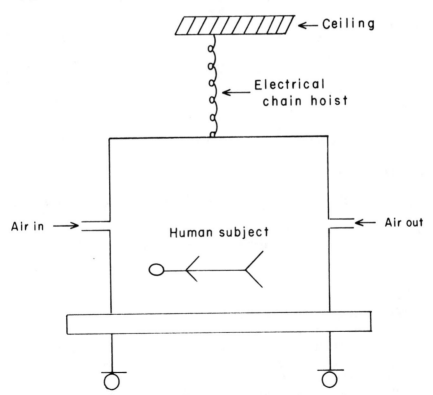

Figure 7-1. A New Design for a Whole-Body Calorimeter to Measure Heat Generation from Human Subjects

Thermal Analysis of the Calorimeter

Calibration Data

The basic transport equation governing the exchange of energy for the whole-body calorimeter (figure 7–1) is

$$\left\{ \begin{array}{c} \text{rate of} \\ \text{energy} \\ \text{in} \end{array} \right\} - \left\{ \begin{array}{c} \text{rate of} \\ \text{energy} \\ \text{out} \end{array} \right\} + \left\{ \begin{array}{c} \text{rate of} \\ \text{energy} \\ \text{generation} \end{array} \right\} - \left\{ \begin{array}{c} \text{rate of} \\ \text{energy} \\ \text{depletion} \end{array} \right\} = \left\{ \begin{array}{c} \text{rate of} \\ \text{energy} \\ \text{accumulation} \end{array} \right\}$$

With the notation in figure 7–4, and using these definitions

$Q1$ = enthalpy of the inlet airstream, cal/hr
$Q2$ = enthalpy of the outlet airstream, cal/hr
$Q3$ = heat generated by a heating mantle (used for calibration of the calorimeter), cal/hr
$Q4$ = heat loss from the whole-body calorimeter, cal/hr

we get

$$Q1 - Q2 + Q3 - Q4 = \frac{\partial U}{\partial t} \tag{7.2}$$

where

U = internal energy of the whole-body calorimeter

Equation 7.2 can be rewritten as

$$\dot{m}1 \, Cp1(T1 - T0) - \dot{m}2 \, Cp2(T - T0) + Q3 - (hA + kA/\Delta X)(T - T0)$$

$$= (\varrho i \, Vi \, Cvi + \varrho w \, Vw \, Cvw + \varrho m \, Vm \, Cvm)\frac{\partial T}{\partial t} \tag{7.3}$$

where

$\dot{m}1$ = inlet dry air mass flow rate
$\dot{m}2$ = outlet dry air mass flow rate
$Cp1$ = heat capacity at constant pressure of the inlet airstream
$Cp2$ = heat capacity at constant pressure of the outlet airstream
$T1$ = inlet airstream temperature
$T0$ = ambient temperature surrounding the calorimeter

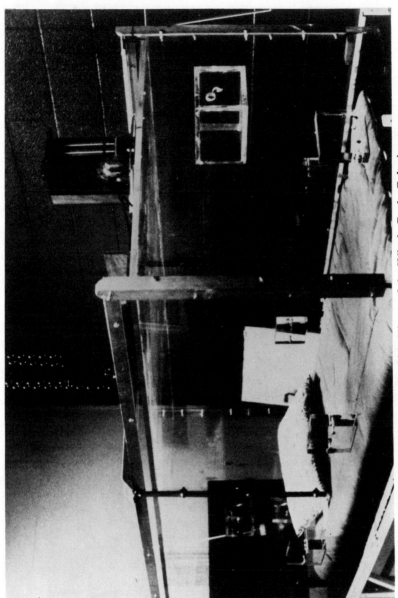

Figure 7-2. Photograph (Side View) of the Whole-Body Calorimeter

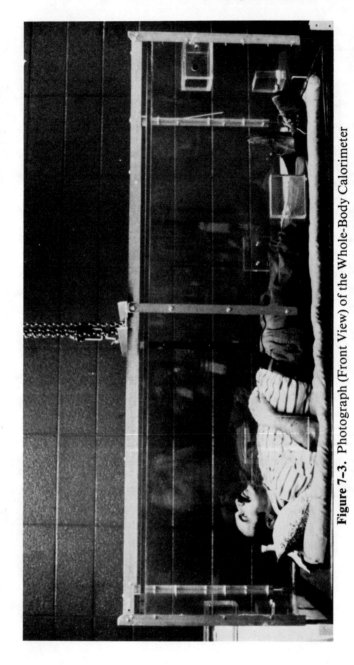

Figure 7-3. Photograph (Front View) of the Whole-Body Calorimeter

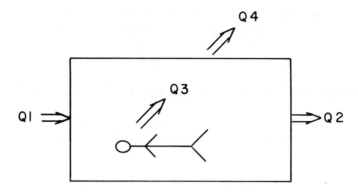

Figure 7–4. Thermal Analysis of the Whole-Body Calorimeter when a Human Subject Is Lying Inside It

T = outlet airstream temperature
ϱi = density of the air inside the calorimeter
ϱw = density of the wall material of the calorimeter
ϱm = density of the heating mantle (used in the calibration studies)
Vi = inside volume of the calorimeter
Vw = volume of the wall material of the calorimeter
Vm = volume of the heating mantle inside the calorimeter (where it is used in the calibration studies)
Cvi = heat capacity at constant volume of the air inside the calorimeter
Cvw = heat capacity at constant volume of the calorimeter wall material
Cvm = heat capacity at constant volume of the heating mantle inside the calorimeter
k = thermal conductivity of the calorimeter wall material
h = convective heat transfer coefficient for heat loss from the calorimeter to its surroundings
A = calorimeter area for heat loss by conduction and convection
ΔX = wall thickness of the calorimeter

Because the temperature rise of the airstream from inlet to outlet is only a few degrees (Fahrenheit), we can assume

$$\dot{m}1\, Cp1 \cong \dot{m}2\, Cp2 \cong \dot{m}\, Cp \qquad (7.4)$$

Let us define α, β, and γ as follows:

$$\alpha = hA + kA/\Delta X \qquad (7.5)$$
$$= \text{first calibration constant for the calorimeter}$$

$$\beta = \varrho i \, Vi \, Cvi + \varrho w \, Vw \, Cvw + \varrho m \, Vm \, Cvm \tag{7.6}$$
$$= \text{second calibration constant for the calorimeter}$$

$$\gamma = \dot{m} \, Cp \tag{7.7}$$

Substituting equations 7.5 through 7.7 into equation 7.3, we obtain

$$\gamma(T1 - T) - \alpha(T - T0) = \beta \, dT/dt$$

or

$$dT/dt + (\frac{\alpha + \gamma}{\beta})T = (\alpha T0 + \alpha T1 + Q3)/\beta \tag{7.8}$$

Let

$$P = \frac{\alpha + \gamma}{\beta} \tag{7.9}$$

$$W = (\alpha T0 + \gamma T1 + Q3)/\beta \tag{7.10}$$

Substituting equations 7.9 and 7.10 into equation 7.8, we can get

$$dT/dt + PT = W \tag{7.11}$$

Equation 7.11 can be solved with its initial condition

$$\text{IC} \qquad T = T0 \qquad \text{at } t = 0 \tag{7.12}$$

to obtain

$$T(t) = (T0 - W/P) \exp(-Pt) + W/P \tag{7.13}$$

For long times, $t \to \infty$, we get from equation 7.13

$$T_\infty = W/P \tag{7.14}$$

where T_∞ represents the temperature of the outlet airstream at steady state and constant $Q3$.

Substituting equation 7.14 into 7.13 and with some rearrangement, we get

$$\ln(T_\infty - T) = \ln(W/P - T0) - Pt \tag{7.15}$$

During the calibration experiment, $T0$, $T1$, T_∞, T, and $Q3$ are measured as a function of time, t. From the slope of the plot of $\ln(T_\infty - T)$ versus t, that is, $-P$, P can be calculated. Thus with known P and T_∞, from equation 7.14 W can be obtained. Gamma can be calculated from our experimental conditions as shown below:

Let

$$\dot{m} = \dot{m}1 = \dot{m}2$$
$$= (35 \text{ l/min}) (60 \text{ min/hr}) (1/28.32 \text{ ft}^3/\text{l}) (0.074 \text{ lb m/ft}^3)$$
$$= 5.487 \text{ lb m/hr dry air} \qquad (7.16)$$

then

$$\gamma = \dot{m}\,Cp = (5.487 \text{ lb m/hr}) (0.25 \text{ Btu/lb m } °\text{F})$$
$$= 1.37 \text{ Btu/hr } °\text{F} \qquad (7.17)$$

With known γ, $Q3$, P, and W, equations 7.9 and 7.10 can be rearranged to give

$$\beta = (-\gamma\,T0 + \gamma\,T1 + Q3)/(W - P\,T0) \qquad (7.18)$$

$$\alpha = P\beta - \gamma \qquad (7.19)$$

and thus we can determine β then α, that is, the two calibration constants required during the experiments with human subjects. Thus equations 7.18 and 7.19 are the working equations for the calibration experiments.

During the calibration experiments, we put a heating mantle in the calorimeter. The heating mantle was connected to an adjustable powerstat and wattmeter. With fixed $\dot{m}$ and γ, for constant $Q3$ (adjusted by the powerstat and wattmeter), we measured $T0$, $T1$, and T at 5-minute intervals for the first hour. Then additional data were obtained every hour for the next 5 hours.

From equations 7.14, 7.15, 7.18, and 7.19 and with our original data, we can get P, W, and the two calibration constants α and β. In appendix C, we present one sample calculation of P, W, α, and β from calibration experiment data. The results of fifteen calibration runs are summarized in table 7–1.

The calibration curve for the SKAN-FLO flowmeter (tube number 1/4-36-6-7; float number Bj-8; SCH 74-62328) used to measure the airflow rate into the whole-body calorimeter is shown in figure 7–5.

Basal Metabolic Rate Measurement of a Human Subject

During the human subject experiments, $T0$, $T1$, and $T(t)$ are measured. Using the experimental data and equation 7.13, the slope of the plot of $T(t)$

Table 7-1
Calibration Constants for the Whole-Body Calorimeter, Calculated from Calibration Experiments

Run #	α Btu/hr°F	β Btu/°F	γ Btu/hr°F	P 1/hr	W °F/hr
1	39.18	45.05	1.37	0.90	69.4
2	40.60	40.70	1.37	1.03	79.9
3	39.20	41.00	1.37	0.99	77.9
4	39.70	45.60	1.37	0.90	71.1
5	38.90	49.70	1.37	0.81	64.4
6	40.20	42.40	1.37	0.98	78.5
7	40.30	37.50	1.37	1.11	89.7
8	37.01	53.75	1.37	0.72	55.09
9	44.66	55.18	1.37	0.82	62.95
10	36.95	41.25	1.37	0.93	72.97
11	40.62	44.91	1.37	0.94	73.87
12	37.10	43.72	1.37	0.88	70.00
13	39.03	40.56	1.37	1.00	79.73
14	39.24	46.41	1.37	0.88	70.70
15	41.78	37.52	1.37	1.15	93.04

αav. $= 39.57 \pm 1.73 = 39.57 \pm 4.37\%$

βav. $= 44.59 \pm 4.96 = 44.39 \pm 11.2\%$

γav. 1.37

Pav. $= 0.936 \pm 0.109 = 0.936 \pm 11.2\%$

Wav. $= 73.95 \pm 9.46 = 73.95 \pm 12.8\%$

versus $\exp(-Pt)$, that is, $T0 - W/P$, can be obtained. Since P is known from previous calibration measurements, W can be calculated. The rate of heat given off from the human body in the basal state, $Q3$, can be calculated from a rearranged form of equation 7.10, that is

$$Q3 = W\beta - \alpha T0 - \gamma T1 \qquad (7.20)$$

(α and β may change slightly since the heating mantle and human body have different dimensions and thermal capacities.)

The basal metabolic rate, (BMR)exp, of the human subject can be obtained as follows:

$$(BMR)exp = Q3 + Qv \qquad (7.21)$$

where

$Q3$ = net rate of body heat released to surroundings

Qv = rate of latent heat absorbed as a result of water evaporation from the skin and the internal surfaces of the body

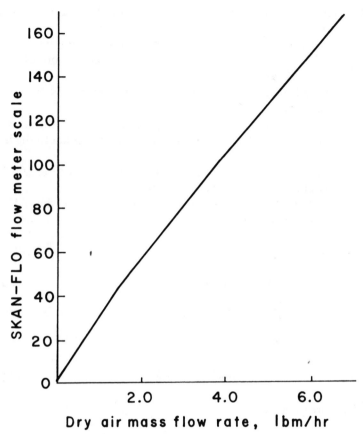

Note: The SKAN-FLO flowmeter is used to measure the air Flow rate into the whole-body calorimeter.

Figure 7-4. Calibration Curve for the SKAN-FLO Flowmeter

The Qv quantity can be calculated as shown below.
Let

Π = barometric pressure
$Td1$ = inlet dry-bulb air temperature
$Td2$ = outlet dry-bulb air temperature
$Ps1$ = vapor pressure of water at $Td1$
$Ps2$ = vapor pressure of water at $Td2$
$Hr1$ = relative humidity inside the calorimeter at the beginning of the measurement and equal to the inlet air humidity

$Hr2$ = relative humidity inside the calorimeter at the end of the measurement

$Pw1$ = partial pressure of water inside the calorimeter at the beginning of the measurement and equal to the partial pressure of water in the inlet air

$Pw2$ = partial pressure of water inside the calorimeter at the end of the measurement

$Z1$ = pounds of water vapor per pound of dry air inside the calorimeter at the beginning of the measurement and equal to the inlet air value

$Z2$ = pounds of water vapor per pound of dry air inside the calorimeter at the end of the measurement

ΔHv = average heat of vaporization of water between $Td1$ and $Td2$

$\dot{m}$ = mass flow rate of dry air

We know that

$$Pw1 = Ps1 \times Hr1 \tag{7.22}$$

$$Pw2 = Ps2 \times Hr2 \tag{7.23}$$

$$Z1 = Pw1/(\Pi - Pw1) \tag{7.24}$$

$$Z2 = Pw2/(\Pi - Pw2) \tag{7.25}$$

and can therefore calculate Qv as

$$Qv = \dot{m}(Z2 - Z1)(\Delta Hv) \tag{7.26}$$

Thus equations 7.20 through 7.26 are the working equations for human subject experiments.

Experimental Procedure

During the basal metabolic experiments, α, β, and γ are known. First, we measured the human subject's height and weight. Then the BMR measurements are made, under uniform conditions [31] such as:

1. The subject has not been exercising for a period of 30 to 60 minutes prior to the measurement.
2. The subject is in a state of absolute mental and physical rest but awake (the sympathetic nervous system is not overactive).

3. The subject must not have eaten anything during the last 12-hour period prior to the measurement (proteins need up to 12 hours to be completely metabolized).
4. The ambient air temperature must be comfortable, 62 to 87°F (which prevents stimulation of the sympathetic nervous system).
5. The subject must have a normal body temperature of 98.6°F.
6. The pulse rate and respiration must be below 80 beats per minute and 25 cycles per minute, respectively.
7. The subject should wear a loose-fitting gown to keep the same experimental conditions each time.

During the measurements, the subject reclines comfortably in the whole-body calorimeter (see figure 7–3). Temperature-controlled air enters and leaves at a moderate velocity. The one-piece calorimeter top can be raised or lowered by an electrical-chain hoist attached to the ceiling. An airtight seal is made with the stationary bottom section.

We took measurements of $T0$, $T1$, and $T(t)$ every 5 minutes until 40 minutes had elapsed, as illustrated in appendix B where one example of a typical experiment is shown. We also measured dry-bulb temperature and relative humidity at the beginning and at the end of the experiment and thereby calculated Qv. From equations 7.20 through 7.26, we can calculate the (BMR)exp of human subjects in their basal state. One sample calculation is shown in appendix B.

The thermometers used to measure $T0$, $T1$, and T have an accuracy to 0.1°F. Thus the readings of $T0$, $T1$, and T have a relative accuracy of about ±0.2 percent. The α value has about a ±4.4 percent relative accuracy, and the β value, about a ±11.2 percent. From equation 7.20, we can estimate that the $Q3$ value has about a ±12 percent relative accuracy. The Qv value has about a ±5 percent relative accuracy. Therefore from equation 7.21, we can estimate that the (BMR)exp value has about a ±17 percent accuracy.

Appendixes

Appendix A
Sample Calculation of Expected Lifespan, Total Rate of Change of Entropy in the Vicinity of Death, and the Polynomial Regression Equation of (dS/dt)std for Human Males Based on Du Bois's Basal Metabolic Rate Data

Assume the discrete data of (dS/dt)std for human males based on Du Bois's basal metabolic rate data (see table 6-9) can be represented by a second-order polynomial equation. Thus we get

$$(dS/dt)\text{std} = b_0 + b_1 t + b_2 t \qquad t > 16 \qquad \text{(A.1)}$$

To find b_0, b_1, and b_2, we get the following equation based on a polynomial regression technique [82].

$$
\begin{bmatrix}
n & \sum\limits_{j=1}^{n} t_j & \sum\limits_{j=1}^{n} t_j^2 \\
\sum\limits_{j=1}^{n} t_j & \sum\limits_{j=1}^{n} t_j^2 & \sum\limits_{j=1}^{n} t_j^3 \\
\sum\limits_{j=1}^{n} t_j^2 & \sum\limits_{j=1}^{n} t_j^3 & \sum\limits_{j=1}^{n} t_j^4
\end{bmatrix}
\begin{bmatrix}
b_0 \\
b_1 \\
b_2
\end{bmatrix}
$$

$$
=
\begin{bmatrix}
\sum\limits_{j=1}^{n} [(dS/dt)std]_j \\
\sum\limits_{j=1}^{n} [(dS/dt)std]_j \, t_j \\
\sum\limits_{j=1}^{n} [(dS/dt)std]_j \, t_j^2
\end{bmatrix}
\qquad \text{(A.2)}
$$

where

n = total number of discrete data

t_j = age in years

$[(dS/dt)std]_j$ = standard total rate of change of entropy at age t_j, Kcal/Kg hr °K

We choose the following data from table 6–9 to find b_0, b_1, and b_2.
$t_1 = 16$; $t_2 = 18$; $t_3 = 20$; $t_4 = 30$; $t_5 = 40$; $t_6 = 50$; $t_6 = 60$; $t_8 = 70$; $t_9 = 80$.

$[(dS/dt)std]_1 = 3.8852E\text{–}3$; $[(dS/dt)std]_2 = 3.5570E\text{–}3$; $[(dS/dt)std]_3 = 3.3735E\text{–}3$

$[(dS/dt)std]_4 = 3.2016E\text{–}3$; $[(dS/dt)std]_5 = 3.1427E\text{–}3$; $[(dS/dt)std]_6 = 3.0939E\text{–}3$

$[(dS/dt)std]_7 = 2.9940E\text{–}3$; $[(dS/dt)std]_8 = 2.9029E\text{–}3$; $[(dS/dt)std]_9 =$

Substituting the above data t_j and $[(dS/dt)std]_j$ of Table 6–9 into equation A.2 we get

$$
\begin{pmatrix}
9 & 384 & 20880 \\
384 & 20880 & 1304928 \\
20880 & 1304928 & 87880512
\end{pmatrix}
\begin{pmatrix}
b_0 \\ b_1 \\ b_2
\end{pmatrix}
=
\begin{pmatrix}
29.0128E\text{–}3 \\
1179.7532E\text{–}3 \\
62231.4792E\text{–}3
\end{pmatrix}
$$

Thus

$$
\begin{pmatrix}
b_0 \\ b_1 \\ b_2
\end{pmatrix}
=
\frac{\text{adj}
\begin{pmatrix}
9 & 384 & 20880 \\
384 & 20880 & 1304928 \\
20880 & 1304928 & 87880512
\end{pmatrix}}
{\det
\begin{pmatrix}
9 & 384 & 20880 \\
384 & 20880 & 1304928 \\
20880 & 1304928 & 87880512
\end{pmatrix}}
\begin{pmatrix}
29.0128E\text{–}3 \\
1179.7532E\text{–}3 \\
62231.4792E\text{–}3
\end{pmatrix}
$$

$$
=
\frac{
\begin{pmatrix}
1.3211E+11 & -6.4990E+9 & 6.5118E+7 \\
-6.4990E+9 & 3.5495E+8 & -3.7264E+6 \\
6.5118E+7 & -3.7264E+6 & 4.0464E+4
\end{pmatrix}
\begin{pmatrix}
29.0128E\text{–}3 \\
1179.7532E\text{–}3 \\
62231.4792E\text{–}3
\end{pmatrix}}
{5.2934E+10}
$$

$$
=
\frac{
\begin{pmatrix}
2.1805E+8 \\
-1.7000E+6 \\
1.1158E+4
\end{pmatrix}}
{5.2934E+10}
=
\begin{pmatrix}
4.1194E\text{–}3 \\
-3.2119E\text{–}5 \\
2.1079E\text{–}7
\end{pmatrix}
$$

So we have

$$(dS/dt)std = 4.1194E\text{–}3 - (3.2119E\text{–}5)t + (2.1079E\text{–}7)t^2 \qquad t > 16 \tag{A.3}$$

From equation A.1, we obtain

$$\frac{d}{dt}(dS/dt)\text{std} = b_1 + 2b_2 t \qquad (A.4)$$

Thus we can obtain the expected lifespan, $t_{f,\text{std}}$, by setting (d/dt) $[(dS/dt)\text{std}]$ to zero. This gives

$$0 = b_1 + 2b_2 t_{f,\text{std}}$$

Rearranging the above equation, we obtain

$$t_{f,\text{std}} = -b_1/2b_2 \qquad (A.5)$$

Substituting b_1 and b_2 values obtained previously, we have

$$t_{f,\text{std}} = -b_1/2b_2 = (3.2119\text{E}+2)/(2 \times 2.1079)$$
$$= 76.2 \text{ years}$$

Substituting 76.2 for t into equation A.3, we obtain

$$(dS/dt)_{t_{f,\text{std}}} = 2.8957\text{E-3 Kcal/Kg hr °K}$$

Appendix B
Sample Calculation of Basal Metabolic Rate, Entropic Age, Expected Lifespan of Human Subjects, and Total Rate of Change of Entropy in the Vicinity of Death

Date: 11–18–75
Human subject index: F5–1
Chronological age: 65.83 years
Height: 157.48 cm
Weight: 56.72 Kg
Barometric pressure (Π): 742.0 mmHg
Dry air flow rate: ($\dot{m}$): 5.487 lb m/hr

Temperature Measurements

Time (t) Min.	Inlet Temp ($T1$) °C	Outlet Temp (T) °F	Ambient Temp ($T0$) °F
5	24.7	77.30	76.8
10	24.7	77.65	76.8
15	24.7	77.90	76.8
20	24.7	78.10	76.8
25	24.7	78.30	76.8
30	24.7	78.48	76.8
35	24.7	78.58	76.8
40	24.7	78.68	76.8

The plot of $T(t)$ versus t is shown in figure B-1.

$T1$, avg $= 24.7°C = 76.46°F$ $Hr1 = 38$ percent
$T0$, avg $= 76.8°F$ $Hr2 = 42$ percent
$Td1 \quad = 76.5°F$
$Td2 \quad 78.8°F$

The slope of $T(t)$ versus $\exp(-pt)$ and $Q3$ can be calculated from the following program:

```
C     MAIN PROGRAM
      DIMENSION   T(10),X(10),Y(10)
  888 CONTINUE
```

129

```
    READ(5,11,END = 999) T0,T1
 11 FORMAT(2F10.2)
    READ(5,12) (T(I),Y(I),   I = 1,8)
 12 FORMAT(8(F2.0,F8.2))
    SUMX = 0
    SUMY = 0
    SUMXY = 0
    SUMXSQ = 0.
    DO   20     I = 1,8
    X(I) = 1./(EXP(T(I)*.934/60))
    SUMX = SUMX + X(I)
    SUMY = SUMY + Y(I)
    SUMXY = SUMXY + X(I)*Y(I)
    SUMXSQ = SUMXSQ + X(I)**2
 20 CONTINUE
    SLOPE = (8.*SUMXY – SUMX*SUMY)/(8.*SUMXSQ – SUMX**2)
    WRITE(6.30) SLOPE
 30 FORMAT(15x, 'SLOPE = ',F5.2)
    W = 0.934*(TO-SLOPE)
    ALPHA = 39.57
    BETA = 44.39
    GAMMA = 1.37
    QZ 3 = W*BETA – ALPHA* – GAMMA*T1
    WRITE(6,40)     Q3
 40 FORMAT(//,5x,'Q3 = ',F4.0)
    GO TO 888
999 STOP
    END
```

The output of the above program gives us

$$\text{Slope} = -3.57 \tag{7.13}$$

$$Q3 = 187 \text{ Btu/hr} \tag{7.20}$$

Based on equations 7.20 through 7.26, we obtain

$Ps1$	$= 23.36 \text{ mmHg at } Td1 = 76.5°F \text{(see [73])}$
$Pw1$	$= Ps1\, Hr1$ (7.22)
	$= (23.36) \times (0.38) = 8.8768 \text{ mmHg}$
$Z1$	$= Pw1/(\Pi - Pw1)$ (7.24)
	$= 8.8768/(742.0 - 8.8768)$
	$= 0.0121 \text{ 1bm } H_2O/1\text{bm dry air}$

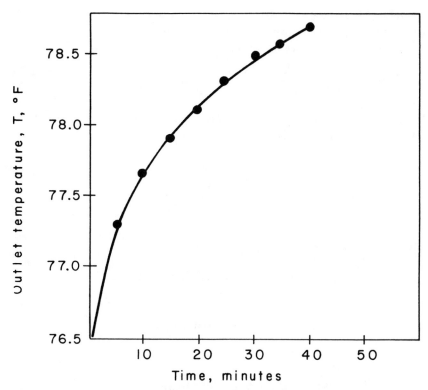

Figure B-1. Outlet Temperature of the Whole-Body Calorimeter: Changes with Time for the Human Subject F5-1's Basal Metabolic Rate Measurement

$Ps2$ = 24.54 mmHg at $Td2$ = 78.8°F(see [73])

$Pw2$ = $Ps2 \times Hr2$ (7.23)

             = (24.54) × (0.42) = 10.3068 mmHg

$Z2$ = $Pw2/(\Pi - Pw2)$ (7.25)

             = 10.3068/(742.0 − 10.3068)

             = 0.0141 1bm H_2O/1bm dry air

ΔHv = 1049.95 Btu/1bm (see [73])

Qv = $\dot{m}(Z2 - Z1)(\Delta Hv)$ (7.26)

             = 5.487(0.0141 − 0.0121)(1049.95)

             = 11.5 Btu/hr

(BMR)exp = $Q3 + Qv$ (7.21)

             = 187 + 11.5 = 198.5 Btu/hr

             = (198.5 × 0.252)/(56.72)

             = 0.8819 Kcal/Kg hr

where 0.252 is the conversion factor from Btu to Kcal and 56.72 is the weight in kilograms of the human subject in figure B-1.

Thus, from equation 6.14 we obtain

$$(d_iS/dt)\exp = (BMR)\exp/T_B$$
$$= 0.8819/309.8 = 2.8467E\text{-}3 \text{ Kcal/Kg hr } °K$$

(6.14)

From table 6.16, we can obtain (BMR)std, d_eS/dt, (dS/dt)std, and $A1$ by linear interpolation, that is

$$(BMR)\text{std} = 0.8421 \text{ Kcal/Kg hr}$$
$$(d_eS/dt) = -0.0416E\text{-}3 \text{ Kcal/Kg hr } °K$$
$$(dS/dt)\text{std} = 2.6767E\text{-}3 \text{ Kcal/Kg hr } °K$$
$$A1 = \int_0^{CA}(dS/dt)\text{std } dt = 1852.4848 \text{ Kcal/Kg } °K$$

From equation 6.2 we obtain

$$(dS/dt)\exp = (d_iS/dt)\exp + d_eS/dt$$
$$= 2.8467E\text{-}3 + (-0.0416E\text{-}3)$$
$$= 2.8051E\text{-}3 \text{ Kcal/Kg hr } °K$$

(6.2)

So

$$k1 = (dS/dt)\exp/(dS/dt)\text{std}$$
$$= (2.8051E\text{-}3)/(2.6767E\text{-}3) = 1.0480$$

(6.26)

Thus

$$A = \int_0^{EA}(dS/dt)\text{std } dt = k1 \times A1$$
$$= (1.0480) \times (1852.4848) = 1941.4041 \text{ Kcal/Kg } °K$$

(6.28)

$$Af = \int_0^{t_f}(dS/dt)\text{std } dt = K/k1$$
$$= (2551.7511)/(1.0480) = 2434.8770 \text{ Kcal/Kg } °K$$

(6.27)

From table 6.16, we can obtain EA and t_f by linear interpolation, that is,

$$EA = 69.63 \text{ years}$$
$$t_f = 91.08 \text{ years}$$

The standard total rate of change of entropy in the vicinity of death, $(dS/dt)_{t_f,\text{std}}$, can be obtained from table 6–16 by interpolation. Thus the total rate of change of entropy in the vicinity of death, $(dS/dt)_{t_f,\text{exp}}$, can be obtained from equation 6.26.

$$
\begin{aligned}
(dS/dt)_{t_f,\text{exp}} &= k1\,(dS/dt)_{t_f,\text{std}} \\
&= (1.0480)(2.6035\text{E--}3) \qquad\qquad (6.26) \\
&= 2.732\text{E--}3 \text{ Kcal/Kg hr } ^\circ\text{K}
\end{aligned}
$$

Appendix C
Sample Calculation for
Calibration Constants
Alpha and Beta

Run #: 1
SKAN-FLO flowmeter setting: 141
Dry air flow rate ($\dot{m}$): 5.487 1bm/hr (see figure 7–3)
$Q3 = 50$ watts $= 171$ Btu/hr
$\gamma = 1.37$ Btu/hr °F (see table 7–1)

Temperature Measurements

Time t	Inlet Temp T1, °F	Outlet Temp T, °F	Ambient Temp T0, °F	$ln(T_\infty - T)$
5 min	72.60	72.15	72.6	1.59939
10 min	72.65	72.65	72.9	1.49290
15 min	72.60	73.10	72.6	1.38629
20 min	72.55	73.40	72.4	1.30833
25 min	72.55	73.70	72.4	1.22378
30 min	72.60	73.80	72.8	1.19392
35 min	72.60	74.05	72.8	1.11514
40 min	72.60	74.35	72.8	1.01160
1 hr	72.65	74.90	72.9	0.78846
2 hr	72.70	76.00	72.9	0.09531
3 hr	72.75	76.65	72.9	−0.79851
4 hr	72.70	77.05	72.9	−2.99573
5 hr	72.70	77.07	72.9	−3.50656

Note: $T_\infty = 77.10°F$; $T1$, avg $= 72.70°F$; $T0$, avg $= 72.9°F$.

The slope of $\ln(T_\infty - T)$ versus $t = -0.90$. From equation 7.15, we get

$$P = 0.90 \text{ hr}^{-1}$$

From equation 7.14, we obtain

$$W = T_\infty \ P$$
$$= (77.10) \times (0.90) = 69.4°\text{F/hr} \tag{7.14}$$

From equation 7.18, we obtain

$$\beta = (-\gamma \ T0 + \gamma \ T1 + Q3)/(W - P \ T0)$$
$$= (-1.37 \times 72.9 + 1.37 \times 72.7 + 171)/(69.4 - 0.9 \times 72.9) \tag{7.18}$$

135

= 170.726/3.79

= 45.05 Btu/°F

From equation 7.19, we obtain

$$\alpha = P\beta - \gamma \qquad\qquad\qquad\qquad (7.19)$$

0.90 × 45.05 − 1.37

= 39.18 Btu/hr°F

Appendix D
Entropy Age and Expected Lifespan Determinations

Entropy age and expected lifespan were determined by using a programmed calculation procedure and precalculated tables (see tables 6–15 and 6–16).

Data Sheet 1

Date: 11–18–75
Human subject index: F5–1
Chronological age: 65.83 years
Name:
Height: 157.48cm (1 in = 2.54 cm)
Weight: 56.72 Kg (1 lbm = 0.454 Kg)
Barometric pressure (Π): 742.0 mmHg
Flowmeter setting: 141
Dry air mass flow rate ($\dot{m}$): 5.487 lbm/hr; T_B = 309.8 K (assumed)

Temperature Measurements

Time t, Min.	Inlet Temp $T1$ °F	Outlet Temp $T(t)$, °F	Ambient Temp $T0$, °F	$exp(-0.936t)$ t, hr
0				
5	76.46	77.30	76.8	0.92496
10	76.46	77.65	76.8	0.85556
15	76.46	77.90	76.8	0.79136
20	76.46	78.10	76.8	0.73198
25	76.46	78.30	76.8	0.67706
30	76.46	78.48	76.8	0.62625
35	76.46	78.58	76.8	0.57926
40	76.46	78.68	76.8	0.53580
45				

$T1$, avg = 76.46 °F; $T0$, avg = 76.8 °F
$Td1 = T1(0) = 76.5$ °F; $Hr1 = Hr(0) = 0.38$
$Td2 = T1(45) = 78.8$ °F; $Hr2 = Hr(45) = 0.42$

Slope can be obtained by plotting the $T(t)$ versus $exp(-0.936t)$ on a regular grid plotting paper.

Slope = -3.52
$Q3 = 0.934(T0,\text{avg} - \text{slope})(44.39) - (39.57)T0,\text{avg} - (1.37)T1,\text{avg}$
$\quad = 9.34(76.8 + 3.52)(44.39) - (39.57)(76.8) - (1.37)(76.46)$
$\quad = 187$ Btu/hr
$Ps1 @ Td1 = 23.36$ mmHg (see Saturated Steam Table)

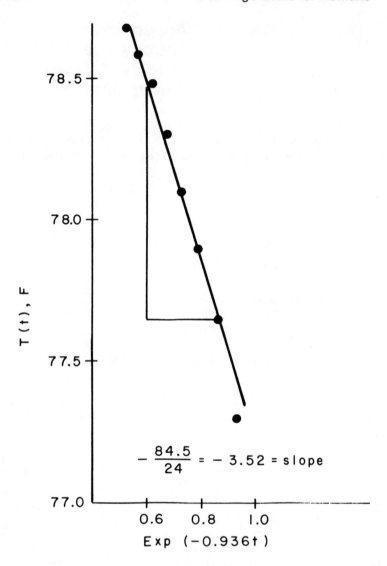

$$-\frac{84.5}{24} = -3.52 = \text{slope}$$

$Ps2 \ @ \ Td2 = 24.54 \ \text{mmHg (see Saturated Steam Table)}$

$\Delta Hv \ @ \ \dfrac{Td1 + Td2}{2} = 1049.95 \ \text{Btu/lbm (see Saturated Steam Table)}$

$Pw1 = Ps1 \times Hr1 = 8.8768 \ \text{mmHg}; \ Pw2 = Ps2 \times Hr2$
$\qquad = 10.3068 \ \text{mm/Hg}$

$Z1 = Pw1/(\Pi - Pw1) = 0.0121; \ Z2 = Pw2/(\Pi - Pw2) = 0.0141$

$Qv = \dot{m}(Z2 - Z1)(\Delta Hv) = 11.5 \ \text{Btu/hr}$

$Q3v = Q3 + Qv = 198.5 \ \text{Btu/hr}$

(BMR)exp = $(0.252)(Q3\,v)$/weight = 0.8819 Kcal/Kg hr
(BMR)std = 0.8678 Kcal/Kg hr (see table 6–15 or table 6–16) for value at CA)

Data Sheet 2

$(d_i S/dt)$exp = (BMR)exp/309.8 = 2.8467×10^{-3} Kcal/Kg hr°K

$(d_e S/dt)$exp = $(d_e S/dt)$std = -0.0416×10^{-3} Kcal/Kg hr °K
   (see table 6–15 or table 6–16 for value at CA)

(dS/dt)exp = $(d_i S/dt)$exp + $(d_e S/dt)$exp = 2.8051×10^{-3} Kcal/Kg hr°K

$(d_i S/dt)$std = 2.7183×10^{-3} Kcal/Kg hr°K
   (see table 6–15 or table 6–16 for value at CA)

(dS/dt)std = 2.6767×10^{-3} Kcal/Kg hr°K
   (see table 6–15 or table 6–16 for value at CA)

$A1 = \int_0^{CA} (dS/dt)\text{std}\,dt = 1852.4848$ Kcal/Kg°K
   (see table 6–15 or table 6–16 for value at CA)

$k1 = (dS/dt)\text{exp}/(dS/dt)\text{std} = \dfrac{2.8051 \times 10^{-3}}{2.6767 \times 10^{-3}} = 1.0480$

$A = \int_0^{EA} (dS/dt)\text{std}\,dt = k1 \times A1 = 1941.4041$ Kcal/Kg°K

$EA = 69.63$ years
   (see table 6–15 or table 6–16 for value at A)

$Af = \int_0^{t_{f,\exp}} (dS/dt)\text{std}\,dt = K/k1 = \begin{cases} 2395/k1 \text{ (males)} \\ 2551/k1 \text{ (females)} \end{cases}$

   $= 2434.8770$ Kcal/Kg°K

$t_{f,\exp}$ = 91.08 years
   (see table 6–15 or table 6–16 for value at Af)

$(dS/dt)_{t_{f,\text{std}}}$ = 2.6035×10^{-3} Kcal/Kg hr°K
   (see table 6–15 or table 6–16 for value at $t_{f,\exp}$)

$(dS/dt)_{t_{f,\exp}}$ = $k1 \times (dS/dt)_{t_{f,\text{std}}}$ = 2.732×10^{-3} Kcal/Kg hr°K

Data Sheet 3

$A1^* = \int_0^{CA} (d_i S/dt)\text{std}\,dt = 1887.6317$ Kcal/Kg°K
   (see table 6–15 or table 6–16 for value at CA)

$k1^* = (d_i S/dt)\text{exp}/(d_i S/dt)\text{std} = 1.0473$

$$A^* = \int_0^{EA^*} (d_i S/dt)\text{std}\, dt = k1^* \times A1^* = 1976.9167 \text{ Kcal/Kg}°\text{K}$$

$EA^* = 69.59$ years

  (see table 6–15 or table 6–16 for value at A^*)

$$Af^* = \int_0^{t^*_{f,\exp}} (d_i S/dt)\text{std}\, dt = K^*/k1^* = \begin{cases} 2456/k1^* \text{ (males)} \\ 2635/k1^* \text{ (females)} \end{cases}$$

$$= 2516.5901 \text{ Kcal/Kg}°\text{K}$$

$t^*_{f,\exp} = 92.79$ years

  (see table 6–15 or table 6–16 for value at Af^*)

$(d_i S/dt)_{t^*_{f,\text{std}}} = 2.610 \text{ Kcal/Kg hr}°\text{K}$

  (see table 6–15 or table 6–16 for value at $t^*_{f,\exp}$)

$(d_i S/dt)_{t^*_{f,\exp}} = k1^* \times (d_i S/dt)_{t^*_{f,\text{std}}}$

$\qquad\qquad = 2.738 \times 10^{-3} \text{ Kcal/Kg hr}°\text{K}$

Exponential Values for Use with Data Sheet

Time (Min.)	$e - 0.936\,(t)^*$
0	1.00000
1	0.98452
2	0.96928
3	0.95428
4	0.93951
5	0.92496
6	0.91065
7	0.89655
8	0.88267
9	0.86901
10	0.85556
11	0.84232
12	0.82928
13	0.81644
14	0.80380
15	0.79136
16	0.77911
17	0.76705
18	0.75518
19	0.74349
20	0.73198
21	0.72065
22	0.70950
23	0.69851
24	0.68770
25	0.67706
26	0.66658
27	0.65626
28	0.64610
29	0.63610
30	0.62625
31	0.61656

(continued)

Time (Min.)	e − 0.936(t)
32	0.60702
33	0.59762
34	0.58837
35	0.57926
36	0.57030
37	0.56147
38	0.55278
39	0.54422
40	0.53580
41	0.52750
42	0.51934
43	0.51130
44	0.50339
45	0.49559

*t, hr

Saturated Steam Table

Temperature t, °F	Absolute Pressure P, mmHg	Specific Latent Heat ΔHv, Btu/lbm
52	9.9162	1063.6
54	10.6659	1062.5
56	11.4724	1061.4
58	12.3254	1060.2
60	13.2405	1059.1
62	14.2125	1057.9
64	15.2465	1056.8
66	16.3478	1055.7
68	17.5162	1054.5
70	18.7570	1053.4
72	20.0754	1052.3
74	21.4713	1051.2
76	22.9551	1050.1
78	24.5268	1048.9
80	26.1967	1047.8
82	27.9649	1046.6
84	29.8416	1045.5
86	31.8114	1044.4
88	33.8898	1043.2
90	36.0871	1042.1

Appendix E
Nomenclature

A = chemical affinity, equation 6.5 a.

A = calorimeter area for heat loss by conduction, equation 7.3.

A $= \int_0^{EA} (dS/dt)\text{std}\, dt = k1\,A1 =$ area under the (dS/dt)std curve up to age EA, equation 6.28.

A^* $= \int_0^{EA^*} (d_iS/dt)\text{std}\, dt = k1^*\, A1^* =$ area under the (d_iS/dt)std curve up to age EA^*, equation 6.31.

Af $= \int_0^{t_f} (dS/dt)\text{std}\, dt = K/k1 =$ area under the (dS/dt)std curve up to age t_f, equation 6.27.

Af^* $= \int_0^{t_f^*} (d_iS/dt)\text{std}\, dt = K^*/k1^* =$ area under the (d_iS/dt)std curve up to age t_f^*, equation 6.32.

$A1$ $= \int_0^{CA} (dS/dt)\text{std}\, dt =$ area under the (dS/dt)std curve up to age CA.

$A1^*$ $= \int_0^{CA} (d_iS/dt)\text{std} =$ area under the (d_iS/dt)std curve up to age CA.

$b_0,\ b_1,\ b_2$ = coefficients of equation A.1.

(BMR)exp   = measured basal metabolic rate, Kcal/Kg hr.

(BMR)std   = standard basal metabolic rate, Kcal/Kg hr, tables 6–15 and 6–16.

$(\text{BMR})_{t_f^*}$ = basal metabolic rate in the vicinity of death, Kcal/Kg hr.

CA = chronological age, years.

Cp = heat capacity of the gas mixture at constant pressure cal/gm°K, equation 6.17.

$Cp1$ = heat capacity at constant pressure of the inlet airstream, cal/gm °K, equation 7.3.

$Cp2$ = heat capacity at constant pressure of the outlet airstream, cal/gm °K, equation 7.3.

Cvi = heat capacity at constant volume of the air inside the calorimeter, cal/gm °K, equation 7.3.

Cvm = heat capacity at constant volume of the heating mantle inside the calorimeter, cal/gm °K, equation 7.3.

E = internal energy of the human system, Kcal, equation 3.2.

EA = entropic age, years, equation 6.25.

$EA*$ = entropic age, years, equation 6.30.

G = Gibbs free energy, Kcal, equation 6.9.

h = convective heat transfer coefficient of heat loss from the calorimeter to its surroundings, Kcal/hr cm^2 °K, equation 7.3.

ΔHv = average heat of vaporization of water between $Td1$ and $Td2$, equation 7.26.

$Hr1$ = relative humidity inside the calorimeter at the beginning of the measurement and equal to the inlet air humidity, equation 7.22.

$Hr2$ = relative humidity inside the calorimeter at the end of the measurement, equation 7.23.

K $= \int_0^{t_{f,\exp}} (dS/dt)\exp\, dt = \int_0^{t_{f,\mathrm{std}}} (dS/dt)\mathrm{std}\; dt = $ lifetime entropy accumulation, Kcal/Kg °K, equation 6.24.

$K*$ $= \int_0^{t_{f,\exp}^*} (d_iS/dt)\exp\, dt = \int_0^{t_{f,\mathrm{std}}} (d_iS/dt)\mathrm{std}\; dt = $ lifetime accumulation of internal entropy generation, Kcal/Kg °K, equation 6.29.

k = thermal conductivity of the calorimeter wall material, Kcal/hr cm °K, equation 7.3.

$k1$ $= (dS/dt)\exp/(dS/dt)\mathrm{std}$, equation 6.26.

$k1*$ $= (d_iS/dt)\exp/(d_iS/dt)\mathrm{std}$, equation 6.31.

$\dot{m}1$ = inlet dry air mass flow rate, lbm/hr, equation 7.3.

$\dot{m}2$ = outlet dry air mass flow rate, lbm/hr, equation 7.3.

N = number of particles in the human system, equation 3.2.

P = pressure, mmHg (millimeters of mercury), equation 6.10.

P $= \dfrac{\alpha + \gamma}{\beta}$, 1/hr, equation 7.9.

P_{i1} = partial pressure of component i in state 1, mmHg, equation 6.17.

P_{i2} = partial pressure of component i in state 2, mmHg, equation 6.17.

$Ps1$ = vapor pressure of water at $Td1$, mmHg, equation 7.22.

$Ps2$ = vapor pressure of water at $Td2$, mmHg, equation 7.23.

$Pw1$ = partial pressure of water inside the calorimeter at the beginning of measurement and equal to the partial pressure of water in inlet air, mmHg, equation 7.22.

$Pw2$ = partial pressure of water inside the calorimeter at the end of measurement, mmHg, equation 7.23.

Qv = rate of latent heat absorbed as a result of water evaporation from the skin and the internal surfaces of the body, Kcal/hr, equation 7.21.

$Q1$ = enthalpy, of the inlet airstream, figure 7-2.

$Q2$ = enthalpy of the outlet airstream, figure 7-2.

$Q3$ = heat generated by a heating mantle (used for calibration of the calorimeter), figure 7-2, or by the human body in the calorimeter.

$Q4$ = heat loss from the whole-body calorimeter, figure 7-2.

$(\partial Q / \partial t)_{T,P}$ = rate of internal heat generation due to the chemical reactions at constant temperature and pressure, Kcal/hr, equation 6.12.

R = gas constant, 1.987 cal/gm-mol °K, equation 6.21.

$(r_j)_{T,P}$ = heat of reaction of the jth reaction at constant temperature and pressure, equation 6.10.

S = entropy of the human system, Kcal/°K, equation 3.2.

S_i = molar entropy of component i, Kcal/gm-mol °K, equation 6.21.

Sm = molar entropy of the ideal gas mixture, Kcal/gm-mol °K, equation 6.21.

$Sm^{(i)}$ = molar entropy of the inspired airstream, at 25°C, 1 atm, equation 6.22.

$Sm^{(e)}$ = molar entropy of the expired airstream, at 36.8°C, 1 atm, equation 6.22.

ΔS_i, mixing = amount of entropy change during mixing from state 1 to state 2 for component i, Kcal/°K, equation 6.17.

Sorg = organizational entropy, Kcal/°K, equation 3.1.

(dS / dt)exp = total rate of change of entropy during the time interval, dt, of a human subject at chronological age, t.

(dS / dt)std = standard total rate of change of entropy during the time interval, dt, of a human subject at chronological age t (from pooled data).

$(dS / dt)_{t_{f,\exp}}$ = total rate of change of entropy in the vicinity of death, Kcal/Kg hr °K, table 6-17.

$(d_e S / dt)$ = rate of change of entropy of the human system due to exchange of entropy with surroundings, Kcal/Kg hr °K, equation 6.22.

$(d_i S / dt)$exp = internal entropy generation rate of a human subject at chronological age, t, Kcal/Kg hr °K, equation 6.29.

$(d_i S / dt)$std = standard internal entropy generation rate of a human subject at chronological age, t, Kcal/Kg hr °K, equation 6.31, from pooled data.

$(d_i S / dt)_{t_{f,\exp}^*}$ = internal entropy generation rate of a human subject in the vicinity of death, Kcal/Kg hr °K, table 6-18.

T = absolute temperature, °K, equation 6.5b.

T = outlet airstream temperature, °K, equation 7.3.

T_B = human body temperature, 309.8 °K, equation 6.14.

$T0$ = ambient temperature surrounding the calorimeter, °K, equation 7.3.

$T1$ = inlet airstream temperature, °K, equation 7.3.

$T1$ = temperature of the mixture in state 1.

$T2$ = temperature of the mixture in state 2, equation 6.17.

t = time, hours, equation 6.1.

t_f = ultimate lifespan of a human subject.

$t_{f,exp}$ = ultimate lifespan of a human subject, defined by d/dt $(dS/dt)_{f,exp}$ = 0, years, table 6-17.

$t_{f,exp}^{*}$ = ultimate lifespan of a human subject, defined by d/dt $(d_iS/dt)_{f,exp}^{*}$ = 0, years, table 6-18.

$t_{f,std}$ = standard lifespan of a human subject, defined by d/dt $(dS/dt)_{f,std}$ = 0, years, table 6-13.

$t_{f,std}^{*}$ = standard lifespan of a human subject, defined by d/dt $(d_iS/dt)_{f,std}^{*}$ = 0, years, table 6-14.

U = internal energy of the whole-body calorimeter, Kcal, equation 7.2.

u = mean metabolic rate, Kcal/hr, equation 3.1.

u/ϱ = measure of the energy cost of carrying the development of an organism from one defined stage to another, equation 3.1.

V = rate of chemical reaction, equation 6.5a.

$\dot{V}$ = volumetric flow rate of inspired and expired air of a human subject, l/min, equation 6.23.

Vi = inside volume of the calorimeter, centimeters, equation 7.3.

Vm = volume of the heating mantle inside the calorimeter, centimeters, equation 7.3.

Vw = volume of the wall material of the calorimeter, centimeters, equation 7.3.

W = $(\alpha T0 + \gamma T1 + Q3)/\beta$, °F/hr, equation 7.10.

y_i = molar fraction of component i in an ideal gas mixture, equation 6.18b.

$Z1$ = pounds of water vapor per pound of dry air inside the calorimeter at the beginning of a measurement and equal to the inlet air value.

$Z2$ = pounds of water vapor per pound of dry air inside the calorimeter at the end of a measurement.

α = first calibration constant for the calorimeter, Btu/hr °F, equation 7.5.

β = second calibration constant for the calorimeter, Btu/ °F, equation 7.6.

γ	$= \dot{m} \, Cp$, Btu/hr °F, equation 7.7.
Δ	= change in property.
Π	= barometric pressure, mmHg, equation 7.24.
ϱ	= maturation rate for a definitive stage of development of an organism, equation 3.1.
ξ_j	= extent of the jth chemical reaction, equation 6.8.
ν_{kj}	= stoichiometric coefficient of the jth chemical species in the kth chemical reaction, equation 6.5c.
μ_{kj}	= chemical potential of the jth chemical species in the kth chemical reaction, equation 6.5c.

References

[1] Bafitis, H., and Sargent, F., "Human Physiological Adaptability through the Life Sequence," *J. Gerontol.* 32, no. 4 (1977): 402–410.

[2] Bell, R.; Davidson, H.; and Scarborough, M.; *Textbook of Physiology and Biochemistry,* 7th ed. (London: Livingstone, 1968).

[3] von Bertalanffy, L.V., "The Theory of Open Systems in Physics and Biology," *Science* 111 (1950): 23–29.

[4] Birren, J.E., *Handbook of Aging and the Individual* (Chicago: University of Chicago Press, 1976).

[5] Bjorkerud, S., "Isolated Lipofuscin Granules: A Survey of a New Field," *Adv. Gerontol. Res.* 1 (1964): 257–288.

[6] Bolz, R.E., and Tuve, G.L., *Handbook of Tables for Applied Engineering and Science,* 2d ed. (Cleveland: Chemical Rubber Corporation, 1976).

[7] Brandfonbrener, M.; Landowne, M.; and Shock, N.W.; "Changes in Cardiac Output with Age," *Circulation* 12 (1955): 557–566.

[8] Brillouin, L., *Am. Sci.* 37 (1949): 554.

[9] Broda, E., *The Evolution of the Bioenergetic Processes* (New York: Pergamon Press, 1975).

[10] Burch, P.R.J., *An Inquiry Concerning Growth, Disease, and Aging* (Edinburgh: Oliver and Boyd, 1968).

[11] Burnet, F.M., "Some Mutation and Chronic Disease," *Brit. Med. J.* 1 (1965): 338–342.

[12] Ibid., *Intrinsic Mutagenesis: A Genetic Approach to Aging* (New York: Wiley, 1974).

[13] Calloway, N.O., "Heat Production and Senescence," *J. Am. Geriatr. Soc.* 22, no. 4 (1974): 149–150.

[14] Church, R.B., and McCarthy, B.J., "Ribonucleic Acid Synthesis of RNA during Embryonic Liver Development and Its Relationship to Regenerating Liver," *J. Mol. Biol.* 23 (1967): 477–496.

[15] Comfort, A., *Aging: The Biology of Senescence* (New York: Holt, Rinehart & Winston, 1964).

[16] Curtis, H.J., "Biological Mechanisms Underlying the Aging Process," *Science* 141 (1963): 686–694.

[17] Cutler, R.G., "Redundancy of Information Content in the Genome of Mammalian Species as a Protective Mechanism Determining Aging Rate," *Mech. Aging Dev.* 2 (1974): 381–408.

[18] Daniel, C., "Cell Longevity in vivo," in Finch, C.E., and Hayflick, L., eds., *Handbook of the Biology of Aging* (Chicago: Van Nostrand, 1976).

[19] Davies, D.F., and Shock, N.W., "Age Changes in Glomerular Filtration Rate, Effective Renal Plasma Flow, and Tubular Excretory Capacity in Adult Males," *J. Clin. Inves.* 29 (1950): 496–507.

[20] DeGoot, S.R., and Mazur, P., *Non-Equilibrium Thermodynamics* (New York: Interscience, 1961).

[21] Donnelly, R.J.; Herman, R.; and Prigogine, I.; *Non-Equilibrium Thermodynamics Variational Techniques and Stability* (Chicago: University of Chicago Press, 1965).

[22] Faseb, H., "Respiration and Circulation," Federation of American Societies for Experimental Biology (Bethesda, 1971).

[23] Finch, C.E., "Enzyme Activities, Gene Function, and Aging in Mammals," *Exp. Gerontol.* 7 (1972): 53–57.

[24] Frazier, J.M., and Yang, W.K., 'Isoaccepting Transfer Ribonucleic Acids in Liver and Brain of Young and Old BC3F Mice," *Arch. Biochem. Biophys.* 153 (1972): 610–618.

[25] Gatlin, L., *Information Theory and the Living System* (New York: Columbia University Press, 1972).

[26] Gershon, H., and Gershon, D., "Detection of Inactive Enzyme Molecules in Aging Organisms," *Nature* 227 (1970): 1214–1217.

[27] Ibid., "Inactive Enzyme Molecules in Aging Mice: Liver Aldolase," *Proc. Nat. Acad. Sci.* (U.S.) 70 (1973): 909–913.

[28] Georgescu-Roegen, N., *The Entropy Law and the Economic Process* (Cambridge, Mass.: Harvard University Press, 1971).

[29] Ibid., *Energy and Economic Myths* (New York: Pergamon, 1976).

[30] Glansdorf, P., and Prigogine, I., *Thermodynamics of Structure, Stability and Fluctuations* (New York: Wiley-Interscience, 1971).

[31] Guyton, A.C., *Textbook of Medical Physiology,* 4th ed. (Philadelphia: Saunders, 1971).

[32] Haase, R., *Thermodynamics of Irreversible Processes* (Reading, Mass.: Addison-Wesley, 1968).

[33] Hamilton, T.H., "Control by Estrogen of Genetic Transcription and Translation," *Science* 161 (1968): 649–661.

[34] Hart, R.W., and Setlow, R.B., "Correlation between Deoxyribonucleic Acid Excision-Repair and Life-span in a Number of Mammalian Species," *Proc. Nat. Acad. Sci.* (U.S.) 71 (1974): 2169–2173.

[35] Haskins, A.L., "Adjunctive Estrogen Therapy," *Obstet. Gynec.* 11 (1958): 49–58.

[36] Hayflick, L., "The Limited in vitro Lifespan of Human Diploid Cell Strains," *Exp. Cell. Res.* 37 (1965): 614–636.

[37] Hershey, D., "Entropy, Basal Metabolism and Life Expectancy," *Gerontologia* 7 (1963): 245–250.

[38] Ibid., *Lifespan and Factors Affecting It* (Springfield, Ill.: Charles C. Thomas, 1974).

[39] Hershey, D., and Wang, H.H., "Measuring the Rate of Living of the Human Organism by Entropic Analysis," Annual Meeting of the American Aging Association (New York, October 1977).

[40] Hoffman, J.L., and McCay, M.T., "Stability of the Nucleoside Composition of t-RNA during Biological Aging of Mice and Mosquitos," *Nature* 249 (1974): 558–559.

[41] Jones, D.D., "Entropic Models in Biology: The Next Scientific Revolution," *Perspectives Biol. Med.* (Winter, 1977): 285–299.

[42] Kaplan, H.G., and Hreshyshen, M.M., "Gas-Liquid Chromatographic Quantitation in Urinary Estrogens in Nonpregnant Women, Postmenopausal Women and Men," *Am. J. Obstet. Gyn.* 111 (1971): 386–390.

[43] Kleiber, M., *The Fire of Life* (New York: John Wiley & Sons, Inc., 1961).

[44] Kutschenreuter, P.H., "Weather Does Affect Mortality," *Am. Soc. Heat., Refrig., Air-Cond. Eng. J.* (September 1960): 39–43.

[45] Lepkowski, W., *Chem. Eng. News* (April 16, 1979): 30–33.

[46] Ibid., (November 14, 1979): 18–19.

[47] Morowitz, H.J., *Energy Flow in Biology* (New York: Academic Press, 1968).

[48] Munnell, J.F., and Getty, R., "Rate of Accumulation of Cardiac Lipofuscin in the Aging Canine," *J. Gerontol.* 23 (1968): 154–158.

[49] Nicolis, G., and Prigogine, I., *Self-Organization in Non-Equilibrium Systems* (New York: Wiley, 1977).

[50] Norris, A.H.; Shock, N.W.; and Wagman, I.H.; "Age Changes in the Maximum Conduction Velocity of Motor Fibers of Human Ulnar Nerves," *J. Appl. Physiol.* 5 (1953): 589–593.

[51] Norris, A.H.; Shock, N.W.; Landowne, M.; and Falozone, A., Jr.; "Pulmonary Function Studies: Age Difference in Lung Volumes and Bellows Function," *Gerontology* 11 (1956): 379–387.

[52] Oliviera, R.J., and Pfuderer, P., "Test for Missynthesis of Lactate Dehydrogenase in Aging Mice by Use of a Monospecific Antibody," *Exp. Gerontol.* 8 (1973): 193–198.

[53] Orgel, L.E., "The Maintenance of Accuracy of Protein Synthesis and Its Relevance to Aging," *Proc. Nat. Acad. Sci.* (U.S.) 49 (1963): 517–521.

[54] Ibid., "Maintenance of the Accuracy of Protein Synthesis and Its Relation to Aging," *Proc. Nat. Acad. Sci.* (U.S.) 67 (1970): 1476.

[55] Peusner, L., *Concepts in Bioenergetics* (Englewood Cliffs, N.J.: Prentice-Hall, 1974).

[56] Prigogine, I., *Etude Thermodynamique des phenomenes irreversibles* (Liege: Desoer, 1947).

[57] Prigogine, I., and Wiame, J.M., *Biologie et thermodynamique des phenomenes irreversibles, Experientia* (Basle) 2 (1946): 451.

[58] Prigogine, I., *Introduction to Thermodynamics of Irreversible Processes* 3d ed. (New York: Interscience Publishers, 1967).

[59] Ibid., "Can Thermodynamics Explain Biological Order?" *Impact Sci. Soc.* 23, no. 3 (1973): 151-179.

[60] Prigogine, I.; Nicolis, G.; and Babloyantz, A.; *Non-Equilibrium Problems in Biological Phenomena* (New York: Interscience, 1975) pp. 99-105.

[61] Prigogine, I., "Time, Structure and Fluctuations," *Science* 201, no. 4359 (September 1978): 777-785.

[62] Rice, N.R., and Straus, N.A., "Relatedness of Mouse Satellite Deoxyribonucleic Acid to Deoxyribonucleic Acid of Various Mouse Species," *Proc. Nat. Acad. Sci.* (U.S.) 70 (1973): 3546-3550.

[63] Rysselberghe, P.V., *Thermodynamics of Irreversible Processes* (Paris: Hermann, 1963).

[64] Sacher, G.A., "The Complementarity of Entropy Terms for the Temperature-Dependence of Development and Aging," *Ann. N.Y. Acad. Sci.* (1968): 681-712.

[65] Samaras, T.T., "The Law of Entropy and the Aging Process," *Human Develop.* 17 (1974): 314-320.

[66] Saunders, J.W., "Death in Embryonic Systems," *Science* 154 (1966): 604-612.

[67] Seyler, L.E., Jr., and Reichlin, S., "Luteinizing Hormone-Releasing Factor (LRF) in Plasma of Postmenopausal Women," *J. Clin. Endocrinol. Metab.* 37 (1973): 197-203.

[68] Shock, N.W., and Yiengst, M.J., "Age Changes in Basal Respiratory Measurements and Metabolism in Males," *J. Gerontol.* 10 (1955): 31-40.

[69] Shock, N.W., "Some of the Facts of Aging," American Association for the Advancement of Science Symposium, no. 65 (Washington, 1960).

[70] Shock, N.W. et al., "Age Differences in the Water Content of the Body Related to Basal Oxygen Consumption in Males," *J. Geronto.* 18 (1963): 1.

[71] Siakotos, A.N., and Koppang, N., "Procedures for the Isolation of Lipopigments from Brain, Heart, and Liver, and Their Properties," *Mech. Aging Dev.* 2 (1973): 177-200.

[72] Simonson, E., *Physiology of Work Capacity and Fatigue* (Springfield, Ill.: Charles C. Thomas, 1971).

[73] Smith, J.M., and Van Ness, H.C., *Introduction to Chemical Engineering Thermodynamics* (New York: McGraw-Hill, 1975).

[74] Metropolitan Life Insurance Company, *Statist. Bull.* 50 (July-September 1978): 8-9.

[75] Strehler, B.L., "Origin and Comparison of the Effects of Time and High Energy Radiations of Living Systems," *Quart. Rev. Biol.* 34 (1959): 117-142.

[76] Strehler, B.L., and Mildvan A.S., "General Theory of Mortality and Aging," *Science* 132 (1960): 14-21.

[77] Swarz, F.J., "The Development in the Human Liver of Multiple Deoxyribose Nucleic Acid (DNA) Classes and Their Relationship to the Age of the Individual," *Chromosoma* 8 (1956): 53-72.

[78] Szilard, L., "On the Nature of the Aging Process," *Proc. Nat. Acad. Sci.* (U.S.) 45 (1959): 30-45.

[79] Terris, M., "Approaches to an Epidemiology of Health," *Am. J. Public Health* 65 (1975): 1037-1045.

[80] Toth, S.E., "The Origin of Lipofuscin Age Pigments," *Exp. Gerontol.* 3 (1968): 19-30.

[81] Tsai, C.C., and Yen, S.S.C., "Acute Effects of Intravenous Infusion of 17 β-Estradiol on Gonadotrophin Release in Pre- and Post-Menopausal Women," *J. Clin. Endocrinol. Metab.* 32 (1971): 766-771.

[82] Walpole, R.E., and Myers, R.H., *Probability and Statistics for Engineers and Scientists* (New York: Macmillan, 1973).

[83] Wheeler, K.T., and Lett, J.T., "On the Possibility that DNA Repair Is Related to Age in Non-Dividing Cells," *Proc. Nat. Acad. Sci.* 71 (1974): 1862-1865.

[84] Williamson, A.R., and Askonas, B.A., "Senescence of an Antibody Forming Clone," *Nature* 238 (1972): 337-339.

[85] Yamaji, T., and Ibayashi, H., "Plasma Dehydroepiandrosterone Sulfate in Normal and Pathological Conditions," *J. Clin. Endocrinol. Metab.* 29 (79): 273-278.

[86] Zeman, K., *Entropy and Information in Science and Philosophy* (New York: Elsevier, 1975).

Index

About the Authors

Daniel Hershey is professor of chemical engineering and chairman of the Gerontology Council at the University of Cincinnati. He has also served as assistant to the president of the University of Cincinnati. He received the B.S. degree from Cooper Union and the Ph.D. from the University of Tennessee. Dr. Hershey is the author of numerous papers on blood flow and blood oxygenation. His interests for the last six years have been in gerontology, and he has done research in basal metabolism, entropy, and life expectancy as related to dieters, smokers, and joggers. His other areas of research include the study of longevity of corporations and civilizations. Dr. Hershey is past president of the Cincinnati chapter of Sigma Xi, an honorary research society, and of the American Association of University Professors. He is a Fellow of the Graduate School at the University of Cincinnati, a member of the Ohio Network of Educational Consultants on Aging, and the convenor of the Greater Cincinnati Gerontology Consortium.

Hsuan-Hsien Wang is a senior research engineer at the University of Tennessee Space Institute in Tullahoma, where he works on open-cycle coal-burning magnetohydrodynamic power generation. He was born in Taiwan and received the B.S. degree from National Cheng Kung University and the Ph.D. from the University of Cincinnati in 1979.

DATE DUE

DEC 0 8 198			
DEC 0 1 REC'D			
APR 2 5 198			
APR 1 4 REC'D			
GAYLORD			PRINTED IN U.S.A.